INDIAN BASICS

A FIREFLY BOOK

Published by Firefly Books Ltd. 2011

Copyright © 2010 Marabout

First printing

Publisher Cataloging-in-Publication Data (U.S.)
Vassallo, Jody.
      Indian basics : 85 recipes illustrated step by step / Jody Vassallo ; photographs by James Lindsay.
[256] p. : col. photos. ;   cm.
Includes index.
Summary: Photographic, step by step cooking instructions showing ingredients, techniques and finished Indian dishes.
ISBN-13: 978-1-55407-939-1 (pbk.)
1. Cooking -- India. I. Lindsay, James. II. Title.
641.5954 dc22   TX724.5.I4V38   2011

Library and Archives Canada Cataloguing in Publication
Vassallo, Jody
      Indian basics : 85 recipes illustrated step by step / Jody
Vassallo ; photographs by James Lindsay.
(My cooking class)
Includes index.
Translation of: Les basiques indiens.
ISBN 978-1-55407-939-1
      1. Cooking, Indic. 2. Cookbooks. I. Lindsay, James, photographer
II. Title. III. Series: My cooking class
TX724.5.I4V3413 2011   641.5954   C2011-901602-8

Published in the United States by
Firefly Books (U.S.) Inc.
P.O. Box 1338, Ellicott Station
Buffalo, New York 14205

Published in Canada by
Firefly Books Ltd.
66 Leek Crescent
Richmond Hill, Ontario L4B 1H1

Printed in Canada

MY COOKING CLASS

INDIAN
BASICS

85 RECIPES
ILLUSTRATED STEP BY STEP

JODY VASSALLO

PHOTOGRAPHS BY JAMES LYNDSAY

* * *

FIREFLY BOOKS

INTRODUCTION

Preparing an Indian meal need not be a mammoth task. Gone are the days when one would spend an entire day in the kitchen. Modern Indian cooks have taken the basics of Indian cooking and adapted them to our busy lives. Rather than spend countless hours crushing spices, making pastes, arm yourself with a few appliances and make your cooking experience that much more pleasurable.

The most important thing to remember when cooking Indian food is that your spices must be fresh. Spice is everything to an Indian dish. I beg you to take the time to grind your own spices, as these will be the foundation of your recipe and greatly affect a dish's flavor.

Indian cuisine is amazing, and the best way to enjoy it is to cook a couple of dishes and serve with rice, chutney and chapati. Don't worry if you have any leftovers — they taste even better the next day.

The book also includes Ayurvedic charts and recipes. Ayurveda is a traditional Indian medicine that dates back over 5,000 years. According to Ayurveda, our body's constitution is made up of three energies of humors called *dosha*. To keep your *dosha* in balance, there are certain foods that you should eat and others you should avoid. Ayurveda uses food as medicine to keep the body in balance. Throughout this book, a symbol (⌒) indicates which recipes are suitable for an Ayurvedic diet.

Sit down with a pen and paper, make yourself a cup of masala chai and decide what you are going to cook for dinner tonight. *Namaste.*

✳ ✳ ✳

CONTENTS

INDIAN ESSENTIALS

1

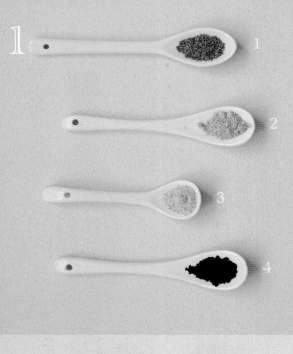

SPICES

❧ A TYPICAL RANGE OF SPICES THAT YOU WILL FIND IN AN INDIAN KITCHEN ❧

1. Ajowan seeds
2. Amchoor powder
3. Asafetida (hing)
4. Black onion seeds (nigella)
5. Black Indian salt (kala namak)
6. Bay leaves

7. Green cardamom pods
8. Ground cardamom
9. Chaat masala
10. Brown cardamom (black cardamom) pods
11. Cinnamon sticks

12. Chili powder
13. Cumin seeds
14. Ground cloves
15. Whole cloves
16. Ground cinnamon

17
18
19
20

21
22

23
24

25
26
27
28

29
30
31
32

17. Ground cumin
18. Curry leaves
19. Coriander seeds
20. Ground coriander
21. Fenugreek leaves
22. Fennel seeds

23. Garam masala
24. Fenugreek seeds
25. Ground ginger
26. Yellow mustard seed
27. Black mustard seed
28. Paprika

29. Black peppercorns
30. Tandoori masala
31. Turmeric
32. Saffron

DAL

➔ THERE ARE NUMEROUS VARIETIES OF DALS IN INDIAN CUISINE ❖

Most dals (also dahl or dhal) benefit from being soaked overnight or for several hours before cooking. Split mung beans, split urid (urad) and red lentils do not need to be soaked first, and they are perfect for a quick-cooking and creamy dal. Cook the dals with a pinch of turmeric and a pinch of salt. The salt adds flavor as does the the turmeric, but it also helps you digest the pulse. Make sure you cook your dal in a large pot with plenty of water, and take care when cooking, as they have a tendency to boil over once they come to a rolling boil. Cooking time for dals may differ slightly from the ones advised in the recipes. Cooking time will

be determined by the freshness of the dal you purchase — the older the dal, the longer it will take to cook. Buy dal from a wholefood store, natural food store or Indian grocery store, which are more likely to have a good turnover of stock.

1. Top, split mung beans, without husks; bottom, split mung beans with husks

2. Yellow split peas, called chana dal

3. Top, black gram beans (urads, urids, black mung beans); bottom, split black gram beans

4. Split orange lentils, called masoor dal

5. Chickpeas (garbanzo beans)

6. Yellow split lentils (split pigeon peas), called toor dal

7. Red kidney beans, called rajma

8. Bengal gram beans (black chickpeas), called kala chana

3

HOW TO MAKE GHEE

❖ MAKES 1 CUP (250 ML) • PREPARATION: 5 MINUTES • COOKING: 15 MINUTES + COOLING ❖

½ pound (250 g) organic butter

3

1
4

2
5

3
6

1	Melt the butter in a small saucepan.	2	Cook, without stirring, until it stops bubbling and the milk solids rise to top.	3	Cool, then strain through cheesecloth to remove the solids.
4	After straining, a clear liquid is left.	5	Transfer the liquid ghee to an airtight container.	6	Store in an airtight container at room temperature. It will thicken as it cools.

HOW TO MAKE PANEER

❧ MAKES 3 CUPS (750 ML) • PREPARATION: 15 MINUTES + STANDING • COOKING: 10 MINUTES ❧

8 cups (2 L) unhomogenized milk
2–3 tablespoons (30–45 ml) lemon juice

1 2
3 4

1	Put the milk into a heavy-bottomed pan and bring it to a boil. Add the lemon juice and stir slowly until it curdles and forms curds and whey.	2	Line a colander with cheesecloth and pour the curds and whey through the colander.
3	Tie the top of the cheesecloth and weigh the mixture down with a can for 30 minutes, or until it is firm. (The longer it's pressed, the firmer it will be).	4	Remove the mixture from the cheesecloth and store it in the refrigerator in an airtight container until you are ready to use it.

HOW TO MAKE GARAM MASALA

❧ MAKES ¾ CUP (75 ML) • PREPARATION: 5 MINUTES • COOKING: NONE ❧

2 cinnamon sticks
2 teaspoons (10 ml) cloves
2 teaspoons (10 ml) black peppercorns
2 teaspoons (10 ml) fennel seeds

2 teaspoons (10 ml) green cardamom pods
2 teaspoons (10 ml) coriander seeds
2 bay leaves

1 2
3 4

1	Roast all the spices in a frying pan until they are fragrant.	2	Transfer the roasted spices to a spice grinder, food processor or mortar.
3	Grind until you have a fine powder, then pass the mixture through a sieve to remove any large pieces.	4	Store the garam masala in an airtight jar.

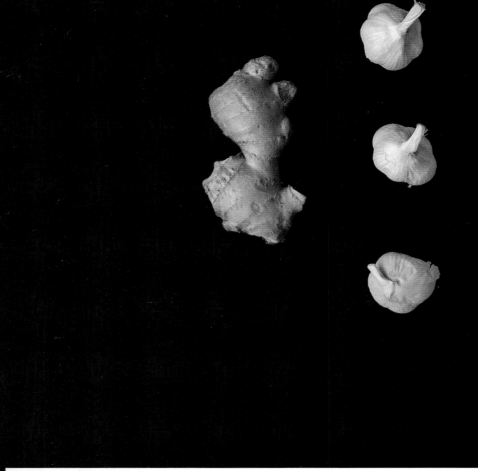

GARLIC-GINGER PASTE

❖ MAKES 7 OUNCES (200 G) • PREPARATION: 20 MINUTES • COOKING: NONE ❖

5 ounces (150 g) fresh ginger
  (about a 10-inch/25 cm piece)
3 small heads garlic (about 40 cloves)

NOTE:
This paste can be kept in the refrigerator for
up to a day. Freeze the rest and thaw in a
bowl of hot water when ready to use. Halve
the recipe if you are only making a couple
of recipes that use it.

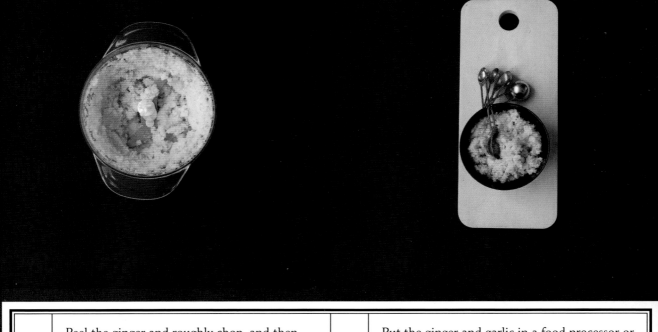

1	Peel the ginger and roughly chop, and then peel the garlic cloves.	2	Put the ginger and garlic in a food processor or spice grinder.
3	Process or grind to form a smooth paste.	4	Transfer the paste into an airtight container and store in the refrigerator (or freezer, if not using within one day).

HOW TO COOK RICE

❖ MAKES 3 CUPS (750 ML) • PREPARATION: 10 MINUTES • COOKING: 20 MINUTES ❖

Ayurvedic

1 cup (250 ml) basmati rice
1 tablespoon (15 ml) ghee
Salt, to taste

1	Put the rice in a colander and rinse it well under cold running water to remove any grit.	2	Put the drained rice in a large pot, cover with water, add the ghee and salt and bring to a boil.
3	Boil, uncovered, until you see tunnels appear in the rice, about 3–5 minutes. Turn the heat to low, cover and cook for 10 minutes.	4	Remove the rice from the heat and allow to stand for about 5 minutes before serving.

HOW TO COOK PAPPADAMS

❖ SERVES 4 • PREPARATION: NONE • COOKING: 5 MINUTES ❖

Sunflower oil, for deep-frying
1 package uncooked pappadams

NOTE:
You can also shallow-fry pappadams in a
frying pan or microwave them following the
instructions on the package.

1	Heat the oil in a large pan to 350°F (180°C), or until a cube of bread browns in 30 seconds.	2	When the oil reaches temperature, add a pappadam and deep-fry until it puffs up. Using tongs, carefully turn the pappadam over once it starts to curl.
3	Remove the cooked pappadam from the pan and drain on paper towels. Repeat with the rest of the pappadams.	4	Serve as a starter to any Indian meal or as an accompaniment to curries.

SOUPS & SNACKS

2

SOUPS

SNACKS

BUTTERNUT SQUASH SAMBAR

Ayurvedic

❖ SERVES 4 • PREPARATION: 30 MINUTES • COOKING: 40 MINUTES ❖

1 cup (250 ml) beans, split mung without husks
½ pound (200 g) butternut squash, peeled and thinly sliced
2 tomatoes, cut into thin wedges
1 teaspoon (5 ml) black mustard seeds

1 tablespoon (15 ml) sunflower oil
2 small red onions, finely chopped
2 garlic cloves, chopped
1 tablespoon (15 ml) grated fresh ginger
1 tablespoon (15 ml) sambar masala (sambar powder)

1 cup (250 ml) tamarind water
1 teaspoon (5 ml) asafetida
Salt, to taste
2 tablespoons (30 ml) chopped fresh cilantro

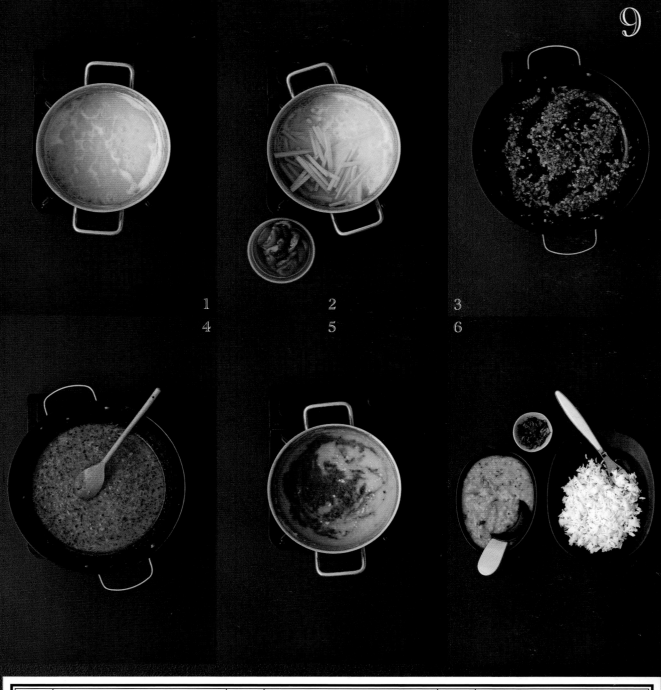

1	Cook the mung beans in 6 cups (1.5 L) of water for 30 minutes, until soft.	2	Add the squash and tomatoes and cook until the squash is soft, adding water if dry.	3	Fry the mustard seeds in the oil until they pop. Fry the onion, garlic and ginger for 5 minutes.
4	Add the sambar powder to the squash mixture and cook for 1 minute. Stir in the tamarind water and bring to a boil.	5	Add squash mixture to the mung beans, add the asafetida and salt and cook until heated through.	6	Stir the cilantro through the sambar and serve with rice.

CARROT & COCONUT SOUP

❧ SERVES 4 • PREPARATION: 30 MINUTES • COOKING: 50 MINUTES ❧

3 tablespoons (45 ml) ghee
1 red onion, halved
2 tablespoons (30 ml) garlic-ginger paste
(see recipe 6)
1½ pounds (750 g) carrots

4 cups (1 L) vegetable stock
1 cup (250 ml) coconut milk
3½ ounces (100 g) paneer, grated (see
recipe 4)
2 tablespoons (30 ml) chopped fresh mint

1   2
3   4

1	Heat the ghee in a pot and fry the onion and garlic-ginger paste until golden brown.	2	Add the carrots and cook until soft. Pour in the stock and coconut milk and stir.
3	Remove the pot from the heat and puree the mixture with a handheld blender until smooth.	4	Pour the soup into bowls, sprinkle the grated paneer and mint on top and serve.

CHOW CHOW BHATH

❖ SERVES 4 • PREPARATION: 15 MINUTES • COOKING: 20 MINUTES ❖

Ayurvedic

2 tablespoons (30 ml) ghee
1 cup (250 ml) coarse semolina
½ teaspoon (2 ml) ground cinnamon
½ teaspoon (2 ml) ground cardamom
½ teaspoon (2 ml) ground cloves

2 cups (500 ml) whole milk (3.5%)
¼ cup (60 ml) jaggery or soft brown sugar
1 teaspoon (5 ml) yellow mustard seeds
6 curry leaves

2 tablespoons (30 ml) split mung beans, without husks
1 tomato, chopped
⅓ cup (75 ml) cashews

1 2
3 4

1	To make a sweet bhath, heat half the ghee in a pan, add half the semolina and all of the ground spices and cook until the semolina is browned and toasted.	2	Add half the milk and half the sugar and cook, stirring constantly, until smooth.	
3	Continue stirring until the mixture boils, thickens and comes away from the sides of the pan.	4	Add the rest of the sugar and stir until it has dissolved. Press the mixture into molds.	➤

5 6
7 8

5	To make the savory bhath, heat the remaining ghee in the cleaned pan, add the mustard seeds and curry leaves and fry until the seeds pop.	6	Add the rest of the semolina and the mung beans and cook over medium heat until toasted.
7	Add the remaining milk and stir until the mixture boils, thickens and comes away from the sides of the pan.	8	Add the tomato and cashews to the semolina mixture and stir to incorporate. Press the mixture into molds.

9 Invert the molds onto serving plates, turn out the bhaths and serve a sweet and savory bhath side by side on a plate. Sprinkle the sweet bhaths with extra ghee, cinnamon and cardamom.

VARIATION
❋

This dish is traditionally served for breakfast in southern India. You can flavor the sweet bhath in various ways, for example, add fresh fruit and use fruit juice instead of the milk.

VEGETABLE & PANEER SAMOSAS

➤ MAKES 12 • PREPARATION: 30 MINUTES + STANDING TIME • COOKING: 1 HOUR ➤

PASTRY:
1 cup (250 ml) all-purpose flour
2 teaspoons (10 ml) fine semolina
Pinch salt
1 tablespoon (15 ml) sunflower oil, plus
    extra for deep-frying

FILLING:
2 tablespoons (30 ml) sunflower oil
⅓ cup (75 ml) peas
½ teaspoon (2 ml) turmeric
1 teaspoon (5 ml) cumin seeds
1 teaspoon (5 ml) ground corianer

1 teaspoon (5 ml) garam masala
½ teaspoon (2 ml) amchoor powder (optional)
¼ teaspoon (1 ml) chili powder (optional)
2 potatoes, peeled, chopped and steamed
3½ ounces (100 g) paneer, grated
    (see recipe 4)

1	Put the flour, semolina and salt in a bowl and make a well in the center.	2	Add the oil and most of ¼ cup (60 ml) lukewarm water and mix with your hands until the dough comes together.	
3	Knead the dough until smooth, cover, then allow to stand for 20 minutes. Divide the dough into 6 pieces and roll into balls.	4	To make the filling, heat the oil in a pan, add the peas, turmeric and cumin seeds and cook until the peas are soft.	➤

5 6
7 8

5	Add the remaining spices and the potatoes and cook until heated through. Remove from the heat and fold the paneer through the mixture.	6	Roll out a piece of the dough to a diameter of 6 inches (15 cm). Cut in half and brush the edges with water. Fold together and seal to form a cone.
7	Fill the cone with potato mixture, fold the top over and seal well. Repeat with remaining dough and filling.	8	Heat the oil for deep-frying in a deep pot and cook the samosas in batches until crisp and golden. Drain on paper towels.

| 9 | Serve the samosas with tamarind chutney (see recipe 68). | Make these samosas in advance and either freeze them or seal in an airtight container and allow to chill in the refrigerator. Thaw or return to room temperature before deep-frying. If you are short on time you can use ready-made shortcrust pastry. |

EGG CHAPATI

❧ SERVES 1 • PREPARATION: 5 MINUTES • COOKING: 10 MINUTES ❧

2 teaspoons (10 ml) sunflower oil
1 tablespoon (15 ml) finely chopped
    red onion
2 eggs

1 tablespoon (15 ml) chopped fresh cilantro
    (optional)
1 whole wheat chapati (packaged or see
    recipe 59)
tomato chutney, to serve

1	Heat the oil in a nonstick frying pan, and fry the onion for 5 minutes.	2	Crack the eggs into the pan and cook until they start to set.	3	Use a plastic fork to break the yolks and sprinkle the cilantro on top.
4	Press the chapati on top of the egg so it sticks.	5	Cook for 3 minutes, until the eggs set, and then turn over and warm the other side of the chapati.	6	Fold the chapati over and serve with tomato chutney (see recipe 69).

POHA

❧ SERVES 4 • PREPARATION: 15 MINUTES • COOKING: 15 MINUTES ❧

Ayurvedic

1 cup (250 ml) beaten (or flattened) rice (poha)
1 teaspoon (5 ml) cumin seeds
1 teaspoon (5 ml) black mustard seeds
2 tablespoons (30 ml) ghee

1 teaspoon (5 ml) turmeric
1 tablespoon (15 ml) sesame seeds
1 potato, peeled and finely diced
1 tablespoon (15 ml) water
Black Indian salt (kala namak)

TO SERVE:
2 tablespoons (30 ml) chopped fresh cilantro
2 tablespoons (30 ml) raw almonds, chopped
Garam masala, to taste
1 lemon, cut into wedges

1	Rinse the rice under cold running water until the water runs clear, and then place it in a bowl and flake with a fork. Set aside.	2	Fry the cumin and mustard seeds in ghee until they pop. Add the turmeric, sesame seeds, potato and water, cover and cook the potatoes until soft.
3	Add the rice and cook for 5 minutes, tossing gently, until the rice is soft and coated in the turmeric-potato mixture. Season with the salt.	4	Serve bowls of poha sprinkled with cilantro, almonds and garam masala. Squeeze the lemon on top just before serving.

ALOO TIKKI

❧ MAKES 12 • PREPARATION: 30 MINUTES • COOKING: 40 MINUTES ❧

1 pound (500 g) potatoes, unpeeled
1 tablespoon (15 ml) sunflower oil, plus
    extra for shallow-frying
2 teaspoons (10 ml) garlic-ginger paste
    (see recipe 6)
½ cup (125 ml) corn kernels

½ teaspoon (2 ml) garam masala
1 tablespoon (15 ml) fresh chopped
    cilantro, plus leaves to garnish
2 tablespoonss (30 ml) water
2 tablespoons (30 ml) cornstarch, for
    dusting

TO SERVE:
Plain yogurt
Pomegranate seeds
Tamarind chutney

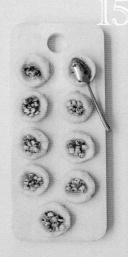

1   2   3
4   5   6

1	Cook the potatoes until soft. Allow to cool slightly then mash.	2	Heat oil, add the paste, corn, garam masala, cilantro and water and fry for 5 minutes.	3	Using lightly oiled hands, shape 1–2 tablespoons (15–30 ml) of the mashed potatoes into flat cakes.
4	Top half the patties with a little corn mix and cover with another patty. Press edges to seal.	5	Coat patties in cornstarch, shaking off excess. Shallow-fry until crisp and golden.	6	Top with cilantro leaves, yogurt, pomegranate seeds and chutney.

PEA & CILANTRO DUMPLINGS

⇥ MAKES 32 • PREPARATION: 30 MINUTES • COOKING: 30 MINUTES ⇤

2 tablespoons (30 ml) ghee
1 cup (250 ml) peas
1 teaspoon (5 ml) cumin seeds
2 teaspoons (10 ml) garlic-ginger paste
 (see recipe 6)

Sea salt, to taste
Pinch of cracked black pepper
2 tablespoons (30 ml) chopped fresh cilantro
3 sheets puff pastry
1 tablespoon (15 ml) milk

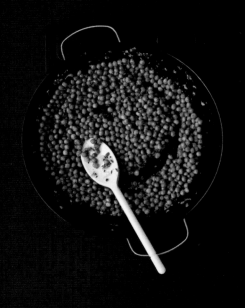

1 2
3 4

1	Preheat oven to 425°F (220°C). Heat the ghee. Add the peas, cumin, paste, salt and pepper and cook until the peas are tender.	2	Remove from the heat and stir in the cilantro.	
3	Roll out the pastry and cut out 2¾-inch (7 cm) circles with a cutter.	4	Spoon 1 teaspoon (5 ml) of filling onto one side of the pastry, brush the edges with water and fold over to enclose the filling.	➢

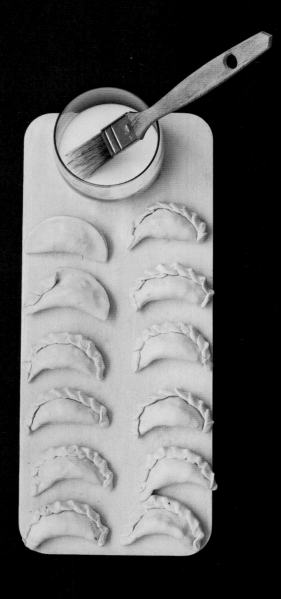

| 5 | Crimp the edges of the pastry to seal tightly. | **TIP**
❋
These make a delicious appetizer, hors d'oeuvre or finger food, especially when served with paneer vegetable samosas (see recipe 12) and with bowls of yogurt topped with tamarind chutney (see recipe 68). |

6	Place on a baking sheet and bake the dumplings for 15–20 minutes, until crisp and golden. Serve with tamarind chutney (see recipe 68) and yogurt, if desired.	**NOTE** ❊ You can bake these dumplings in advance and then freeze them. Thaw and then reheat them in an oven preheated to 350°F (180°C).

PANEER OMELET

❧ SERVES 1 • PREPARATION: 10 MINUTES • COOKING: 10 MINUTES ❧

Ayurvedic

1 tablespoon (15 ml) ghee
1 small red onion, finely chopped
½ teaspoon (2 ml) cumin seeds
1 small ripe tomato, chopped

2 eggs, lightly beaten
1 ounce (30 g) paneer, grated (see recipe 4)
1 tablespoon (15 ml) chopped fresh cilantro

1	Heat the ghee in a nonstick frying pan and fry the onion and cumin seeds for 5 minutes, until golden.	2	Add the tomato and cook until there is no moisture left in the pan.
3	Pour the eggs into the pan. Lift the edge as it sets to allow any unset egg to run underneath.	4	Sprinkle with the paneer and cilantro and allow to set before serving.

DALS & VEGETABLES

DALS

VEGETABLES

3

SPINACH DAL

❧ SERVES 4 • PREPARATION: 15 MINUTES • COOKING: 40 MINUTES ❧

Ayurvedic

½ cup (125 ml) split mung beans,
    without husks
½ cup (125 ml) split orange lentils
4 cups (1 L) water
1 teaspoon (5 ml) turmeric

½ teaspoon (2 ml) sea salt
1 tablespoon (15 ml) ghee
1 small red onion, finely chopped
1 ripe tomato, chopped

1 garlic clove, sliced
1 green chili, sliced into rings (optional)
1 teaspoon (5 ml) cumin seeds
2 cups (500 ml) chopped spinach

1   2
3   4

1	Wash the beans under cold running water three times, until the water runs clear.	2	Transfer to a pot and add the water. Bring to a boil, add the turmeric and salt and cook for 20 minutes.
3	Heat the ghee in a frying pan, add the onion and cook for 5 minutes, until golden brown.	4	Add the tomato, garlic, chili and cumin seeds, and stirfry until cooked through. ➤

5	Add the spinach and cook for 5 minutes, until the spinach is soft.	**TIP** ✻
		Be sure to cook the dal until it is soft and creamy. If you cannot find split mung dal use split orange lentils or split black gram beans instead.

6	Fold the vegetable mixture into the dal. Add a little of the mixed dal to the frying pan and stir to remove any sediment from the bottom of the pan. Return this bit of dal to the pot. Taste and adjust the seasoning as desired. Serve.

NOTE
❄

The secret to a good dal is the seasoning. Cook the spice mix (called tarka) until the spices are fragrant and the onions are soft and sweet. Finish the dal with a generous pinch of good-quality salt.

CHOLE

➤ SERVES 4 • PREPARATION: 20 MINUTES + OVERNIGHT SOAKING • COOKING: 1 HOUR ➤

1 cup (250 ml) dried chickpeas
6 cups (1.5 L) water
2 tablespoons (30 ml) ghee
1 red onion, finely chopped
1 teaspoon (5 ml) cumin seeds

1 teaspoon (5 ml) garam masala
½ teaspoon (2 ml) black pepper
1 teaspoon (5 ml) turmeric
1 teaspoon (5 ml) ground ginger

10 ounces (300 g) ripe tomatoes, chopped
 (about 1 cup/250 ml)
1 cup (250 ml) finely shredded cabbage
1½ cups (375 ml) milk
2 tablespoons (30 ml) chopped cilantro

1 2
3 4

1	Soak the chickpeas overnight. Drain them and put them into a pot. Cover with the water and boil for 40 minutes, until soft.	2	Heat the ghee in a frying pan and fry the onion for about 5 minutes, until golden. Add the spices and fry for 2 minutes, until fragrant.
3	Drain the chickpeas and add to the pan along with the tomatoes, cabbage and milk. Bring to a boil then reduce the heat and cook for 20 minutes.	4	Add the cilantro and serve with raita (see recipe 73).

PUNJABI BLACK GRAM BEAN DAL

❧ SERVES 4 • PREPARATION: 20 MINUTES + OVERNIGHT SOAKING • COOKING: 50 MINUTES ❧

¾ cup (175 ml) black gram beans	1 brown cardamom pod, lightly crushed	2 whole cloves
4 cups (1 L) water	1 cinnamon stick	½ teaspoon (2 ml) ground ginger
1 green chili, halved lengthwise	10 ounces (300 g) tomatoes, chopped	3 tablespoons (45 ml) ghee
¼ teaspoon (1 ml) turmeric	½ cup (125 ml) light cream (20%)	1 teaspoon (5 ml) cumin seeds

1   2   3
4   5   6

1	Soak the beans overnight. Drain and put in a pot with the water.	2	Add the chili, turmeric, cardamom and cinnamon and cook until the beans are soft.	3	Remove the cardamom pods and cinnamon stick and lightly mash the beans.
4	Add tomatoes, cream, cloves and ginger. Bring to a boil then simmer for 20 minutes.	5	Heat the ghee in a frying pan and fry the cumin seeds until browned.	6	Pour the cumin and ghee over the dal and serve with salad and raita. (see recipe 73)

RAJMA

✦ SERVES 4 • PREPARATION: 15 MINUTES • COOKING: 1½ HOURS ✦

Ayurvedic

1½ cups (375 ml) red kidney beans (rajma)
10 cups (2.5 L) water
1 pound (500 g) tomatoes, chopped (about
    1½ cups/375 ml)
1 tablespoon (15 ml) chopped fresh ginger
2 garlic cloves

1 green chili, halved lengthwise
1 red onion, chopped
1 tablespoon (15 ml) sunflower oil
1 teaspoon (5 ml) cumin seeds
Pinch of asafetida

½ teaspoon (2 ml) turmeric
1 teaspoon (5 ml) garam masala
½ teaspoon (2 ml) chili powder
Sea salt, to taste
2 tablespoons (30 ml) chopped fresh cilantro

1	Soak the beans overnight in 7 cups (1.75 L) of water, then drain them and put them into a pot with the water. Boil for 40 minutes, until soft. Drain.	2	Put the tomatoes, ginger, garlic, chili and onion into a blender or food processor and blend until smooth.	
3	Heat the oil in a pan, and fry the cumin seeds and asafetida until the seeds pop. Add the pureed tomato and cook, stirring, until thick.	4	Add the turmeric, garam masala, chili powder, salt, beans and the remaining 3 cups (750 ml) of water. Bring to a boil then simmer for 30 minutes.	➤

| 5 | Mash the beans roughly with a potato masher or the back of a spoon. | **TIP** ❋ The beans need to be cooked until soft. The cooking time will vary depending on how fresh the beans are. Cook them in plenty of water on a steady boil. |

| 6 | Sprinkle the cilantro on top and serve with freshly cooked rice. | **VARIATION**
❃
If you are short on time you can use canned red kidney beans instead and omit step 1. Drain them well before using and add them to the onion mixture at step 4. |

COLOR DAL

❖ SERVES 4 • PREPARATION: 20 MINUTES + 2 HOURS SOAKING • COOKING: 1 HOUR ❖

½ cup (125 ml) yellow split peas
½ cup (125 ml) split mung beans,
   without husks
½ cup (125 ml) split orange lentils
½ cup (125 ml) black gram beans
½ cup (125 ml) yellow split lentils

5 cups (1.2 L) water
½ teaspoon (2 ml) turmeric
½ teaspoon (2 ml) salt
Pinch of garam masala
Fenugreek leaves, to taste

TARKA:

2 tablespoons (30 ml) ghee
3 garlic cloves, chopped
1 red onion, chopped
1 teaspoon (5 ml) cumin seeds
2 large dried red chilies
2 ripe tomatoes, chopped

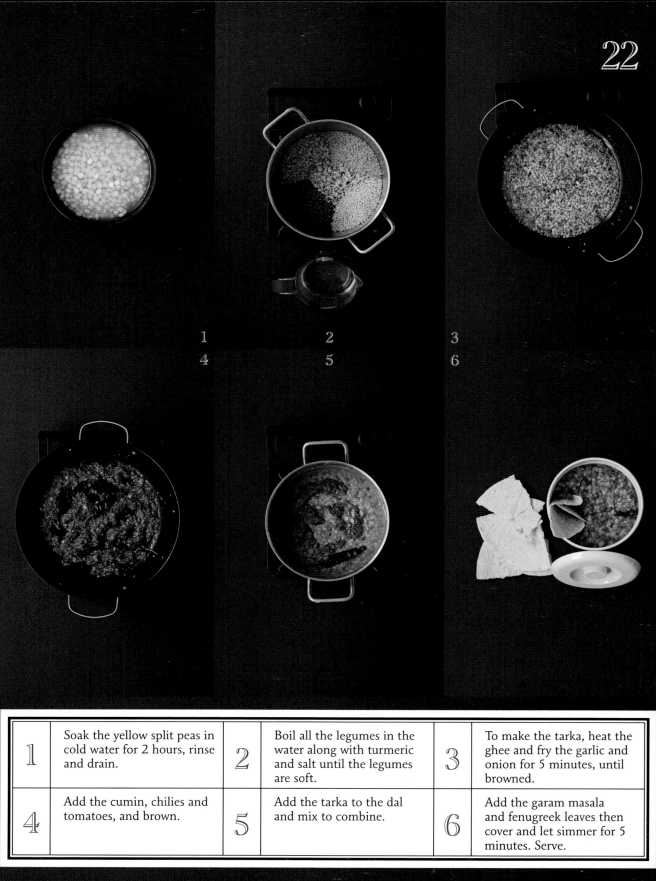

1	Soak the yellow split peas in cold water for 2 hours, rinse and drain.	2	Boil all the legumes in the water along with turmeric and salt until the legumes are soft.	3	To make the tarka, heat the ghee and fry the garlic and onion for 5 minutes, until browned.
4	Add the cumin, chilies and tomatoes, and brown.	5	Add the tarka to the dal and mix to combine.	6	Add the garam masala and fenugreek leaves then cover and let simmer for 5 minutes. Serve.

BUTTERNUT SQUASH THOREN

❖ SERVES 4 • PREPARATION: 30 MINUTES + 2 HOURS SOAKING • COOKING: 30 MINUTES ❖

½ cup (125 ml) yellow split peas
1–2 tablespoons (15–30 ml) sunflower oil
2 tablespoons (30 ml) garlic-ginger paste
  (see recipe 6)
1 red onion, finely chopped
1 teaspoon (5 ml) black mustard seeds
1 teaspoon (5 ml) fenugreek seeds

1 teaspoon (5 ml) cumin seeds
1 tablespoon (15 ml) roughly chopped
  curry leaves
1 green chili, halved
½ teaspoon (2 ml) sea salt, plus extra
  to season

1 teaspoon (5 ml) turmeric
1 pound (500 g) butternut squash, cut into
  matchsticks
1 cup (250 ml) coconut milk
1 tablespoon (15 ml) tamarind water
1 cup (250 ml) water

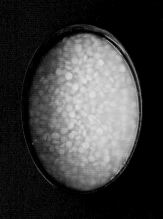

1 2
3 4

1	Soak the split peas in cold water for 2 hours, rinse and drain. Put in a pot, cover with water and boil for 40 minutes, until soft.	2	Heat the oil and fry the garlic-ginger paste and onion until golden brown. Add the mustard seeds, fenugreek, cumin, curry leaves and chili and fry until the seeds pop.
3	Add salt and turmeric, squash, coconut milk, tamarind water and water.	4	Stir in the cooked dal and season with salt to taste. Serve with rice and banana raita (see recipe 73).

BUTTER PANEER

Ayurvedic

❖ SERVES 4 • PREPARATION: 20 MINUTES • COOKING: 40 MINUTES ❖

4 red onions, chopped
1 green chili
1 tablespoon (15 ml) grated fresh ginger
4 tomatoes, roughly diced
3 tablespoons (45 ml) ghee
½ teaspoon (2 ml) turmeric

¼ teaspoon (1 ml) chili powder
½ teaspoon (2 ml) garam masala, plus extra
  to serve
1 cup (250 ml) light cream (20%)
2 tablespoons (30 ml) ground almonds or
  cashews

Sea salt
14 ounces (400 g) paneer, cubed
(see recipe 4)
Fresh cilantro leaves, to serve

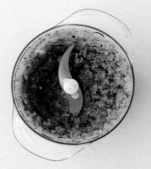

1 2
3 4

1	Process the onions, chili and ginger in a food processor or blender until smooth, adding a little water if needed to help them combine. Set aside.	2	Clean the appliance and puree the tomatoes until smooth. Set aside.	
3	Heat the ghee in a frying pan and brown the spices and onion paste.	4	Add the pureed tomato, cream and ground almonds and cook for a further 5 minutes.	➤

| 5 | Add the paneer, cover and cook for 5 minutes. | **NOTE**
❋
Don't stir the sauce too much after you add the paneer or it may break up into the sauce. Instead, just gently spoon some of the sauce over the paneer to heat it through. |

		TIP ❈
6	Remove from the heat, sprinkle with garam masala and cilantro, season with salt, cover and allow to stand for 5 minutes before serving with poori (see recipe 60) and chutney or raita, such as banana raita (see recipe 73).	The most important thing is to ensure the onions are well cooked, as their sweetness adds a lot of flavor to the dish.

GARLIC-GINGER EGGPLANT

❧ SERVES 4 • PREPARATION: 20 MINUTES • COOKING: 20 MINUTES ❧

24 Japanese or Asian eggplants
12 garlic cloves, chopped
½ cup (125 ml) peeled and chopped
  ginger

2 tablespoons (30 ml) chopped fresh cilantro
1 teaspoon (5 ml) sea salt
Pinch of chili powder (optional)
3 tablespoons (45 ml) sunflower oil

1 2
3 4

1	Cut the eggplants lengthwise into four, being careful not to cut all the way through.	2	Grind the garlic, ginger, cilantro, salt and chili powder, if using, and then rub the mixture into the center of the eggplants and press together.
3	Heat the oil in a large, deep frying pan and brown the eggplants on all sides. Cover and cook for 15 minutes, until soft.	4	Serve as a main course with rice or as an appetizer or hors d'oeuvre if your eggplants are small.

BEET CURRY

⇒ SERVES 4 • PREPARATION: 25 MINUTES • COOKING: 40 MINUTES ⇐

¾ pound (350 g) beets
2 tablespoons (30 ml) sunflower oil
1 teaspoon (5 ml) black mustard seeds
1 teaspoon (5 ml) cumin seeds
½ teaspoon (2 ml) turmeric
1 green chili, thinly sliced

1 tablespoon (15 ml) roughly chopped
  curry leaves
2 tablespoons (30 ml) garlic-ginger paste
  (see recipe 6)
1¾ cups (425 ml) coconut milk

½ cup (125 ml) water
½ cup (125 ml) plain yogurt
1 tablespoon (15 ml) tamarind water
Pinch of sea salt
Pinch of black pepper

1	Peel the beets and cut them into matchsticks.	2	Heat the oil and brown the mustard seeds, cumin, turmeric, chili, curry leaves and garlic-ginger paste.
3	Add the coconut milk and water, cover and cook until the beets are soft.	4	Stir in the yogurt, tamarind water, pepper and cook until heated through. Season and serve with freshly cooked rice and fresh cilantro.

MUSHROOM CURRY

✦ SERVES 4 • PREPARATION: 15 MINUTES • COOKING: 10 MINUTES ✦

10 ounces (300 g) chopped tomatoes
   (about 1 cup/250 ml)
30 small mushrooms
2 tablespoons (30 ml) ghee
1 tablespoon (15 ml) garlic-ginger paste
   (see recipe 6)

1 teaspoon (5 ml) garam masala
1 teaspoon (5 ml) fennel seeds
¼ teaspoon (1 ml) chili powder (optional)
1 teaspoon (5 ml) cumin
1¾ cups (425 ml) coconut milk

½ cup (125 ml) light cream (20%)
1 tablespoon (15 ml) fenugreek leaves
2 tablespoons (30 ml) chopped fresh cilantro
Sea salt, to taste

1 2
3 4

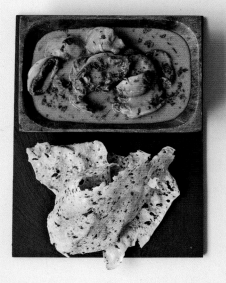

1	Put the tomatoes in a food processor or blender and blend until smooth. Wipe the mushrooms clean using paper towels, trim and slice in half.	2	Heat the ghee and brown the garlic-ginger paste, garam masala, fennel seeds, chili powder, if using, and cumin.
3	Add the mushrooms, coconut milk and pureed tomatoes then bring to a boil. Reduce the heat and simmer for 10 minutes, until heated through.	4	Remove from the heat, stir through the cream, fenugreek and cilantro, season with salt and serve with chapati (see recipe 59).

ALOO GOBI

➤ SERVES 4 • PREPARATION: 20 MINUTES • COOKING: 30 MINUTES ➤

 Ayurvedic

2 tablespoons (30 ml) ghee
1 teaspoon (5 ml) black mustard seeds
1 teaspoon (5 ml) cumin seeds
½ teaspoon (2 ml) turmeric
1 red onion, finely chopped

1 tablespoon (15 ml) garlic-ginger paste
  (see recipe 6)
1 pound (500 g) cauliflower, cut into florets
2 potatoes, peeled and cubed

2 cups (500 ml) water
Chopped cilantro leaves, to garnish
Lemon wedges, to serve

1 2
3 4

1	Heat the ghee, add the mustard and cumin seeds and fry until the mustard seeds pop.	2	Add the turmeric, onion and garlic-ginger paste and stir-fry over a medium heat.
3	Add the cauliflower, potatoes and water, cover and cook for about 15 minutes, until the vegetables are soft.	4	Sprinkle with chopped cilantro and serve with a generous squeeze of lemon and a salad.

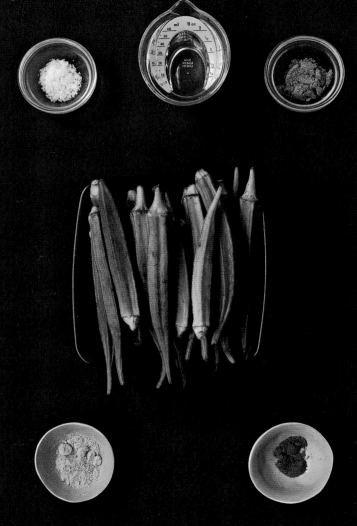

STUFFED OKRA

❧ SERVES 2–6 • PREPARATION: 30 MINUTES • COOKING: 20 MINUTES ❧

24 okra pods
1 teaspoon (5 ml) amchoor powder
¼ teaspoon (1 ml) chili powder

½ teaspoon (2 ml) sea salt
1 teaspoon (5 ml) ground coriander
3 tablespoons (45 ml) sunflower oil

NOTE:
Add a squeeze of lime juice or a little vinegar
to help the okra to stay crisp.

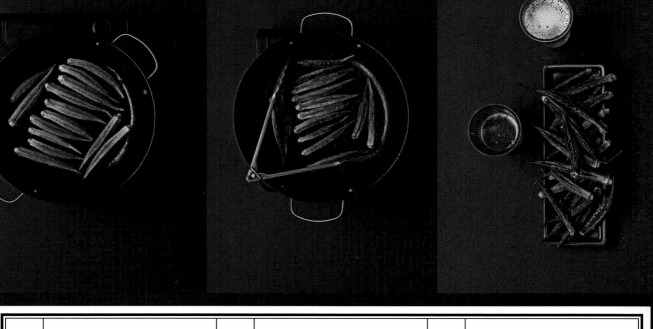

1	Trim the ends from the okra then cut a slit in the center of each pod.	2	Combine the amchoor powder, chili powder, salt and ground coriander.	3	Spoon the mix into the center of each okra pod, press it in and shake off any excess.
4	Heat the oil in a deep pan and brown the okra in batches.	5	Cook until the okra is soft, turning a couple of times to brown all sides.	6	Serve as an hors d'oeuvre or as a side dish with freshly cooked rice and a curry.

MALAI KOFTA

❧ SERVES 4 • PREPARATION: 40 MINUTES • COOKING: 40 MINUTES ❧

1 pound (500 g) potatoes	2 tablespoons (30 ml) ghee	1 red onion, finely chopped	almonds
Sea salt and black pepper, to taste	5 black peppercorns	½ teaspoon (2 ml) turmeric	1 tablespoon (15 ml) coconut
¼ cup (60 ml) raisins, roughly	2 whole cloves	¼ teaspoon (1 ml) chili powder	milk powder
chopped	2 green cardamom pods, lightly	2 tablespoons (30 ml) garlic-	7 ounces (200 g) tomatoes,
¼ cup (60 ml) cashews, roughly	crushed	ginger paste (see recipe 6)	chopped (about ¾ cup/175 ml)
chopped	1 teaspoon (5 ml) fennel seeds	¼ cup (60 ml) water	1 cup (250 ml) milk
2 tablespoons (30 ml) cornstarch	1 cinnamon stick	1 tablespoon (15 ml) ground	Sunflower oil, for shallow-frying

1 2
3 4

1	Boil or steam the potatoes, allow to cool slightly, peel and mash. Season with salt and pepper.	2	Shape 1–2 tablespoons (15–30 ml) of the mashed potato mixture into balls.	
3	Combine the raisins and cashews. Make an indentation into the center of each ball and add 1 teaspoon (5 ml) of the cashew-raisin mixture. Close up the balls fully around the mixture.	4	Roll the balls in cornstarch until well coated, shaking off any excess. Set aside while you prepare the sauce.	➤

5	Heat the ghee in a pan, add the whole spices and brown.	6	Add the onion, ground spices, garlic-ginger paste and water and brown, stirring, until the water has evaporated.
7	Add the almonds, coconut milk powder, tomatoes and milk and bring to a boil. Reduce the heat, cover and simmer for 10 minutes.	8	Heat the oil for shallow-frying and fry the potato balls in batches until crisp and golden.

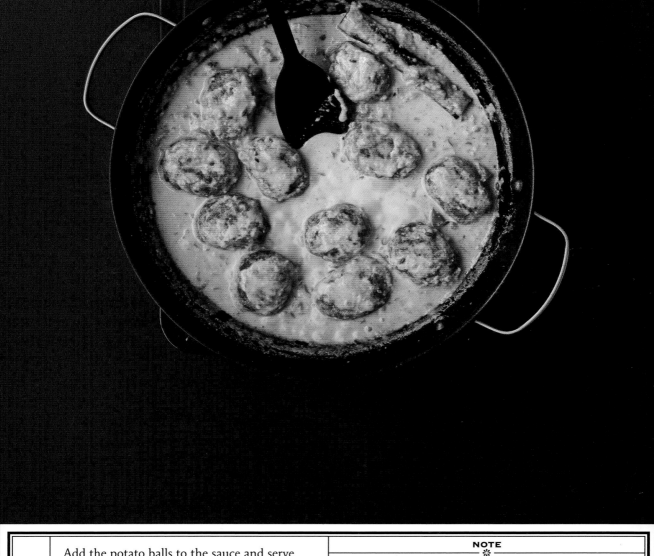

9

Add the potato balls to the sauce and serve while they are still crisp.

INDIAN BAKED VEGETABLE

Ayurvedic

❧ SERVES 4 • PREPARATION: 20 MINUTES • COOKING: 40 MINUTES ❧

1½ pounds (750 g) sweet potatoes, peeled
 and cut into thin wedges
1 red pepper, cut into strips
1 green pepper, cut into strips
1 orange pepper, cut into strips
14 ounces (400 g) cauliflower, cut into florets

1 red onion, cut into thin wedges
7 ounces (200 g) green beans, trimmed
3 tablespoons (45 ml) sunflower oil
1 tablespoon (15 ml) ghee
2 tablespoons (30 ml) garlic-ginger paste
 (see recipe 6)

Pinch of sea salt
1 teaspoon (5 ml) cumin seeds
1 teaspoon (5 ml) turmeric
Pinch of garam masala
1 tablespoon (15 ml) lemon juice

1	Preheat oven to 400°F (200°C). Prepare the vegetables.	2	Combine the oil, ghee, garlic-ginger paste, salt, cumin, turmeric, garam masala and lemon juice in a large bowl.
3	Put all the vegetables except the beans in the bowl and mix well, until coated in the oil. Transfer the vegetables to a large roasting pan.	4	Cook for 35 minutes, then add the beans and continue cooking for 5–10 minutes, or until the vegetables are soft.

PALAK PANEER

Ayurvedic

❧ SERVES 4 • PREPARATION: 20 MINUTES • COOKING: 30 MINUTES ❧

2 pounds (1 kg) spinach leaves, washed
3 tablespoons (45 ml) sunflower oil
1 teaspoon (5 ml) cumin seeds
½ teaspoon (2 ml) fenugreek seeds
2 tablespoons (30 ml) garlic-ginger paste
   (see recipe 6)

2 teaspoons (10 ml) ground coriander
1 cup (250 ml) water
½ cup (125 ml) milk or light cream (20%)
14 ounces (400 g) paneer, cubed
   (see recipe 4)
1 tablespoon (15 ml) ghee

Sea salt, to taste
1 teaspoon (5 ml) garam masala
Grated paneer, to serve

1	Cook the spinach until it wilts, then blend in a food processor or blender until smooth.	2	Heat the oil and brown the cumin and fenugreek seeds.	3	Add the garlic-ginger paste and continue to brown.
4	Add spinach, coriander, water and milk. Cook until thick.	5	Add the paneer and ghee and stir until the ghee melts and the paneer is hot. Season.	6	Add the garam masala, cover and leave for 5 minutes. Top with grated paneer.

VEGETABLE CURRY

❧ SERVES 4 • PREPARATION: 30 MINUTES + OVERNIGHT SOAKING • COOKING: 40 MINUTES ❧

½ cup (125 ml) black chickpeas
2 tablespoons (30 ml) ghee
1 teaspoon (5 ml) cumin seeds
½ teaspoon (2 ml) fennel seeds
½ teaspoon (2 ml) fenugreek seeds
1 tablespoon (15 ml) grated fresh ginger
1 red onion, chopped

Pinch of asafetida
1 small red pepper, chopped
10 ounces (300 g) sweet potato, chopped
   (about 2 cups/500 ml)
1 zucchini, sliced
½ cup (125 ml) peas

14 ounces (400 g) tomatoes, chopped
   (about 1¼ cups/310 ml)
¼ cup (60 ml) water
1 teaspoon (5 ml) garam masala
½ teaspoon (2 ml) turmeric
2 tablespoons (30 ml) plain yogurt
Sea salt, to taste

1	Soak the chickpeas in cold water overnight. Drain and boil in a large pot until tender. Drain and set aside.	2	Heat the ghee and fry the seeds until fragrant. Add the ginger, onion and asafetida and cook until the onion is golden.
3	Add the vegetables, chickpeas, water, garam masala and turmeric and bring to a boil. Reduce the heat and simmer for about 20 minutes.	4	Stir in the yogurt, season with salt to taste and serve with pappadams (see recipe 8).

MUNG BEANS WITH COCONUT

❖ SERVES 4 • PREPARATION: 20 MINUTES + OVERNIGHT SOAKING • COOKING: 40 MINUTES ❖

½ cup (125 ml) whole mung beans, soaked
   overnight then drained
1 cup (250 ml) water
2 tablespoons (30 ml) sunflower oil or ghee

1 teaspoon (5 ml) black mustard seeds
1 teaspoon (5 ml) cumin seeds
1 tablespoon (15 ml) roughly chopped
   curry leaves

1 cup (250 ml) shredded coconut
Pinch of ground black pepper
Sea salt, to taste
Lemon wedges, to serve

1 2
3 4

1	Put the mung beans in a pan with water and boil until just soft. Do not overcook.	2	Heat the oil or ghee and fry the mustard seeds until they start to pop. Add the cumin and curry leaves and cook until fragrant.
3	Stir in the coconut and mung beans and cook until golden.	4	Season with salt and pepper and serve with the lemon wedges.

EGGPLANT KORMA

⟩ SERVES 4 • PREPARATION: 30 MINUTES + 30 MINUTES STANDING • COOKING: 40 MINUTES ⟨

1 pound (500 g) eggplants, chopped (about
   3½ cups/375 ml)
1 teaspoon (5 ml) sea salt
1 tablespoon (15 ml) white vinegar
1 tablespoon (15 ml) sunflower oil
1 teaspoon (5 ml) black mustard seeds

1 tablespoon (15 ml) roughly chopped
   curry leaves
10 ounces (300 g) ripe tomatoes, chopped
   (about 1 cup/250 ml)
1 teaspoon (5 ml) turmeric

½ teaspoon (2 ml) garam masala
½ teaspoon (2 ml) black pepper
1 cup (250 ml) coconut milk
½ cup (125 ml) water
1 tablespoon (15 ml) fenugreek leaves

1	Sprinkle the salt and vinegar on the eggplants and combine. Leave for 30 minutes then drain.	2	Heat the oil and fry the mustard seeds for 2 minutes, until they pop.	3	Add the curry leaves, tomatoes and turmeric and lightly stir-fry.
4	Add the eggplant and combine. Cover and cook until the eggplant is soft.	5	Add the garam masala, pepper, coconut milk and water.	6	Bring to a boil then let simmer for 20 minutes. Sprinkle the fenugreek leaves on top and serve.

VEGETABLE & PANEER KEBABS

❖ MAKES 6 • PREPARATION: 15 MINUTES • COOKING: 20 MINUTES ❖

4 pieces of naan bread
7 ounces (200 g) paneer, cubed (see recipe 4)
2 zucchinis, cut into thick slices
1 red pepper, cubed

1 green pepper, cubed
1 red onion, cut into wedges
12 mushrooms
2 tablespoons (30 ml) ghee, melted

2 garlic cloves, chopped
1 teaspoon (5 ml) garam masala
Sea salt, to taste

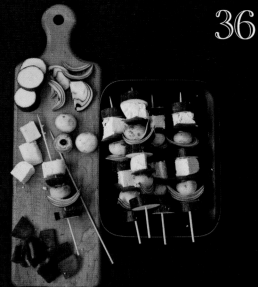

1 2
3 4

1	Light a barbecue or preheat a grill pan and preheat the oven to 350°F (180°C). Wrap the naan bread in foil and place in the oven.	2	Thread the paneer, zucchini, peppers, onion and mushrooms onto presoaked bamboo skewers (see note).
3	Combine the melted ghee, garlic, garam masala and salt.	4	Brush the kebabs with the ghee mixture. ➤

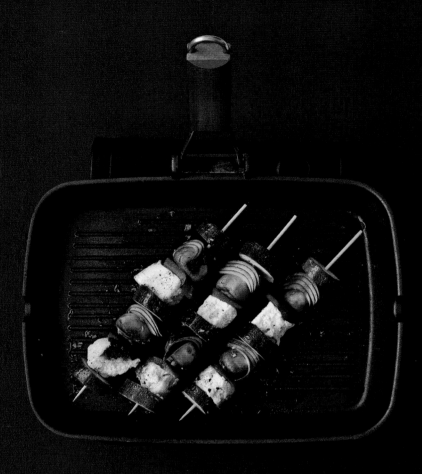

5   Cook the kebabs on a lightly oiled barbecue or in a grill pan until the vegetables are tender.

VARIATION
✿

You can use a variety of vegatables for the kebabs or substitute pieces of chicken or fish for the paneer. Adjust the cooking times accordingly.

6	Serve the kebabs on the warm naan with cilantro & mint chutney (see recipe 71).	see recipe 71

NOTE
❖

Soak the bamboo skewers in cold water for at least 30 minutes before using to prevent them from burning during cooking. You can use metal skewers instead, if you prefer.

CAULIFLOWER & SPINACH CURRY

❧ SERVES 4 • PREPARATION: 20 MINUTES • COOKING: 50 MINUTES ❧

1 pound (500 g) spinach
1 tablespoon (15 ml) garlic-ginger paste
   (see recipe 6)
1 green chili, sliced
1 teaspoon (5 ml) fenugreek leaves

1 cup (250 ml) water
2 tablespoons (30 ml) sunflower oil
1 tablespoon (15 ml) ghee
1 teaspoon (5 ml) cumin seeds
1 teaspoon (5 ml) ground coriander

½ teaspoon (2 ml) turmeric
1 pound (500 g) cauliflower, cut into florets
Sunflower oil, for shallow-frying
Generous pinch of sea salt
Lemon wedges, to serve

1 2
3 4

1	Boil the spinach, garlic-ginger paste, chili, fenugreek leaves and water until the spinach wilts.	2	Drain well then transfer to a blender or food processor and blend until smooth.	
3	Heat the oil and ghee in a pan and fry the cumin, coriander and turmeric until fragrant.	4	Add the spinach mixture to the pan and stir to combine.	➤

			TIP
5	Heat the oil for shallow-frying in a large, deep pan or wok and fry the cauliflower in batches until golden. Drain on paper towels.		If you don't like your dishes too hot, remove the seeds from the chili. When seeding chilies, always wear gloves and wash the knife, cutting board and your hands when finished.

| 6 | Add the cauliflower to the spinach mixture and cook until heated through. Season with salt and serve with lemon wedges. | **NOTE**
✽
This dish also makes an ideal accompaniment to a dal, vegetable curry or meat curry along with freshly cooked rice or chapati (see recipe 59). |

MEAT, EGGS & FISH

4

SPICED LEG OF LAMB

❖ SERVES 4 • PREPARATION: 15 MINUTES + OVERNIGHT MARINATING • COOKING: 1 HOUR ❖

2½ pounds (1.25 kg) leg of lamb
4 garlic cloves
1 cup (250 ml) plain yogurt
1 cup (250 ml) garlic-ginger paste
  (see recipe 6)

1 teaspoon (5 ml) garam masala
½ teaspoon (2 ml) ground ginger
½ teaspoon (2 ml) fennel seeds
½ teaspoon (2 ml) turmeric

4 medium potatoes, peeled and quartered
2 tablespoons (30 ml) sunflower oil
1 tablespoon (15 ml) lemon juice
2 tablespoons (30 ml) chopped fresh cilantro

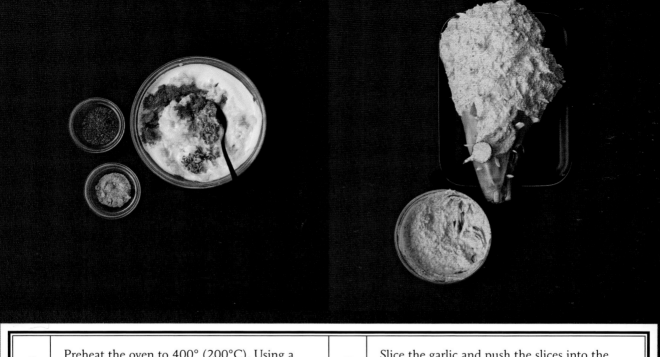

1	Preheat the oven to 400° (200°C). Using a small sharp knife, make small, deep incisions in the top of the lamb.	2	Slice the garlic and push the slices into the incisions in the lamb.	
3	Combine the yogurt, garlic-ginger paste, garam masala, ground ginger, fennel seeds and turmeric.	4	Spread the mixture over the lamb, cover and allow to marinate in the refrigerator overnight.	➤

	Place the lamb on a rack in a roasting pan, arrange the potatoes around it and drizzle with the oil. Bake for 45 minutes, until the lamb is cooked to your liking.	**NOTE** ❋
5		Bring the lamb to room temperature by taking it out of the refrigrator about 30 minutes before putting it into the oven. This will help it cook evenly.

6

Drizzle the potatoes with the lemon juice and cilantro and toss to combine. Slice the lamb and serve with the potatoes.

TIP
❋

Allow 20 minutes of cooking time for every pound (500 g) of lamb for medium rare. Letting the lamb stand before carving ensures the juices remain in the meat rather than ending up on your cutting board.

SHAMI KEBAB

❖ MAKES 12 • PREPARATION: 20 MINUTES + 2 HOURS SOAKING • COOKING: 30 MINUTES ❖

2 tablespoons (30 ml) yellow split peas,
  soaked for 2 hours in cold water then
  drained
1 pound (500 g) ground lamb
3 black peppercorns

2 brown cardamom pods, lightly crushed
2 green cardamom pods, lightly crushed
1 cinnamon stick
3 whole cloves
1 egg white

1 tablespoon (15 ml) grated fresh ginger
1 green chili, chopped
2 tablespoons (30 ml) fresh cilantro,
  chopped
Sunflower oil, for shallow-frying

1 2
3 4

1	Put the split peas, lamb, peppercorns, cardamom, cinnamon and cloves in a pan.	2	Cook, stirring, over medium heat until the lamb is tender and all the moisture has been absorbed. Strain and remove the whole spices.
3	Blend the lamb mixture and egg white in a blender or food processor until smooth. Put in a bowl, add the ginger, chili and cilantro and shape into balls.	4	Heat the oil for shallow-frying and fry the balls in batches until browned on both sides. Allow to cool then serve with chutney (see recipes 67 to 72).

ROGAN JOSH

❖ SERVES 4–6 • PREPARATION: 20 MINUTES + 4 HOURS MARINATING • COOKING: 2 HOURS ❖

1½ pounds (750 g) cubed lamb shoulder
2 tablespoons (30 ml) garlic-ginger paste
  (see recipe 6)
½ cup (125 ml) plain yogurt
1 teaspoon (5 ml) Kashmiri chili powder
2 teaspoons (10 ml) ground cumin
2 teaspoons (10 ml) ground coriander

2 tablespoons (30 ml) ghee
1 red onion, chopped
2 brown cardamom pods, lightly crushed
2 green cardamom pods, lightly crushed
2 bay leaves
6 whole cloves
1 cinnamon stick

1 teaspoon (5 ml) fennel seeds
1 teaspoon (5 ml) salt
½ teaspoon (2 ml) saffron threads
1½ cups (375 ml) water
2 tablespoons (30 ml) fresh cilantro,
  chopped

1	Put the lamb, garlic-ginger paste, yogurt and ground spices in a bowl, cover and marinate for 4 hours.	2	Heat the ghee in a pot and cook the onion over medium heat for 10 minutes, until golden.
3	Add the marinated lamb, spices and water, cover and simmer for 1½ hours, until the lamb is tender.	4	Stir through the chopped cilantro, cover and let stand for 5 minutes. Serve with lime wedges and cilantro leaves.

MINTY LAMB CUTLETS

❖ SERVES 4 • PREPARATION: 15 MINUTES + OVERNIGHT MARINATING • COOKING: 15 MINUTES ❖

8 lamb cutlets
1 small red onion, grated
1 tablespoon (15 ml) finely grated
   fresh ginger
2 garlic cloves, grated

¼ cup (60 ml) mint leaves, chopped
½ teaspoon (2 ml) turmeric
1 teaspoon (5 ml) ground cumin
2 teaspoons (10 ml) grated jaggery or soft
   brown sugar

Juice of 1 lemon
Plain yogurt, to serve
Pomegranate seeds, to serve

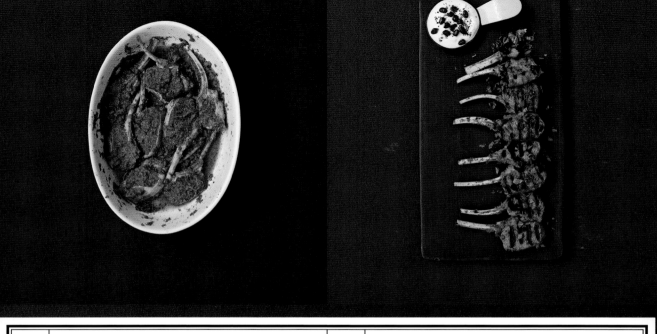

1	Light a barbecue or preheat the grill. Trim the lamb cutlets, removing any unwanted fat and sinew.	2	Blend the onion, ginger, garlic, mint, turmeric, cumin, jaggery and lemon juice in a food processor or blender to make a paste.
3	Put the onion paste in a shallow nonmetallic dish, add the lamb and mix until coated. Cover and chill in the refrigerator overnight.	4	Grill the lamb until tender. Serve with plain yogurt and pomegranate seeds.

LAMB KORMA

❖ SERVES 4–6 • PREPARATION: 20 MINUTES + 2 HOURS MARINATING • COOKING: 1 HOUR ❖

2 pounds (1 kg) cubed leg of lamb
¼ cup (60 ml) plain yogurt
1 tablespoon (15 ml) ground coriander
1 teaspoon (5 ml) ground cumin
½ teaspoon (2 ml) ground cardamom

2 onions, diced
1 tablespoon (15 ml) chopped fresh ginger
3 garlic cloves, peeled
½ cup (125 ml) cashews
3 tablespoons (45 ml) ghee

1 cinnamon stick
½ teaspoon (2 ml) salt
1 (14-ounce/398 ml) can of coconut cream
1 (14-ounce/398 ml) can of crushed tomatoes
½ cup (125 ml) water

1	Combine the lamb, yogurt and spices, cover and leave for 2 hours.	2	Blend half the onion, the ginger, garlic, cashews and a little water until smooth.	3	Heat the ghee and cook the remaining onions for 5 minutes, until golden.
4	Add the lamb and cook for 5 minutes, until the meat changes color.	5	Add the onion-cashew paste and the remaining ingredients.	6	Cover and simmer for 30 minutes, then uncover and let simmer until thick.

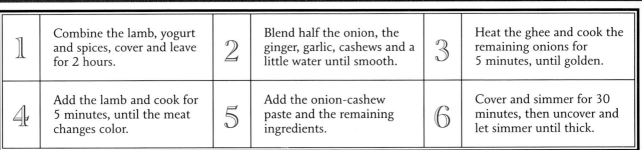

LAMB SAAG

❧ SERVES 4 • PREPARATION: 20 MINUTES • COOKING: 2 HOURS ❧

3 tablespoons (45 ml) ghee
3 onions, diced
1 pound (500 g) spinach, chopped
2 green chilies, sliced
2 garlic cloves, chopped
2 tomatoes, diced

2 whole cloves, lightly crushed
2 teaspoons (10 ml) ground coriander
1 teaspoon (5 ml) garam masala
1 teaspoon (5 ml) turmeric
½ cup (125 ml) light cream (20%)
½ cup (125 ml) water

1½ pounds (750 g) cubed lamb leg
 or shoulder
Juice of 1 lemon
Sea salt, to taste

1 2
3 4

1	Heat the ghee in a pot and cook the onions until golden brown.	2	Add the spinach and chilies and cook for 5 minutes.	
3	Add the garlic, tomatoes, cloves, coriander, garam masala and turmeric and cook for 5 minutes.	4	Stir in the cream and water and cook, stirring, for 5 minutes.	➤

	Add the meat to the pot and bring to a boil. Cover and cook for 1½ hours, until the lamb is tender.	**TIP** ❋
5		Be sure to cut the lamb into even-sized pieces and use lamb leg or shoulder, as both will produce a succulent dish.

		NOTE ❄
6	Stir in the lemon juice and season to taste with salt. Serve.	Cook the lamb slowly, rather than on a rolling boil, and season it well before serving.

MADRAS BEEF & DAL CURRY

❧ SERVES 4–6 • PREPARATION: 20 MINUTES • COOKING: 1 HOUR 20 MINUTES ❧

2 tablespoons (30 ml) sunflower oil
1 red onion, diced
2 garlic cloves, chopped
1 pound (500 g) cubed beef bottom round
1 tablespoon (15 ml) garlic-ginger paste
  (see recipe 6)

½ teaspoon (2 ml) chili powder
2 dried red chilies
½ cup (125 ml) split black gram beans
1 (14-ounce/398 ml) can diced tomatoes
3 whole cloves
1 teaspoon (5 ml) turmeric

2 brown cardamom pods, lightly crushed
3 cups (750 ml) water
3 tablespoons (45 ml) chopped fresh cilantro

1	Heat the oil in a large pot and fry the onion and garlic for 10 minutes, until golden. Add the beef and brown.	2	Add the garlic-ginger paste, chili powder, dried chilies and beans and cook for 3 minutes, until the beans are browned.
3	Stir in the tomatoes, spices and water. Cover and cook for 1 hour, until the meat is tender.	4	Stir in the cilantro and serve with rice, raita (see recipe 73), pickles or chutney (see recipes 67 to 72).

EGG MASALA

❧ SERVES 4–6 • PREPARATION: 15 MINUTES • COOKING: 30 MINUTES ❧

8 eggs
2 tablespoons (30 ml) oil
1 red onion, finely chopped
1 tablespoon (15 ml) garlic-ginger paste
  (see recipe 6)

1 tablespoon (15 ml) ground coriander
1 teaspoon (5 ml) garam masala
½ teaspoon (2 ml) hot chili powder
½ teaspoon (2 ml) turmeric
1 tomato, chopped

½ teaspoon (2 ml) salt
1 cup (250 ml) coconut milk
1 tablespoon (15 ml) tamarind concentrate
½ cup (125 ml) water
1 teaspoon (5 ml) dried fenugreek leaves

1	Cook the eggs in a large pot of gently simmering water for 10 minutes, until hard-boiled. Rinse under cold water and peel.	2	Heat the oil and cook the onion and garlic-ginger paste for 10 minutes, until golden. Add the coriander and cook until fragrant.
3	Add the remaining ingredients except the fenugreek leaves and simmer until the oil rises to the surface.	4	Add the eggs and simmer until heated through, then sprinkle with fenugreek leaves and serve with chapati (see recipe 59) and chutney.

CHICKEN TIKKA WRAPS

➤ **SERVES 4 • PREPARATION: 20 MINUTES + 4 HOURS OR MORE MARINATING • COOKING: 20 MINUTES** ◀

2 pounds (1 kg) boneless, skinless
  chicken thighs
1 tablespoon (15 ml) tandoori masala
1 tablespoon (15 ml) lemon juice
1 teaspoon (5 ml) ground cumin
½ teaspoon (2 ml) garam masala

1 tablespoon (15 ml) grated jaggery or soft
  brown sugar
2 tablespoons (30 ml) garlic-ginger paste
  (see recipe 6)
2 tablespoons (30 ml) chopped fresh cilantro
1 cup (250 ml) plain yogurt

6 chapati (see recipe 59)
1 cup (250 ml) shredded lettuce
2 tomatoes, sliced
1 small red onion, thinly sliced (optional)

1 2
3 4

1	Preheat oven to 350°F (180°C) and cut the chicken into bite-sized pieces.	2	Combine the tandoori masala, lemon juice, spices, jaggery, garlic-ginger paste, cilantro and yogurt.
3	Add the chicken to the marinade, cover and refrigerate for 4 hours or overnight.	4	Cook the chicken under a hot grill for 15 minutes, turning, until tender. ➤

| 5 | Wrap the chapati in foil and warm in the oven for 10 minutes. | **VARIATION**
❋
This chicken is delicious tossed through a simple salad or served with some rice and raitas (see recipe 73). |

| 6 | Serve with the lettuce, tomato, onion and your choice of chutney (see recipes 67 to 72). | **TIP**
❉

These wraps make a great summer evening meal. Put the chicken in the marinade before going to work, then take it out of the refrigerator to bring it to room temperature when you get home. Cook on the barbecue or under a grill. |

GREEN MASALA CHICKEN SALAD

⇥ SERVES 4 • PREPARATION: 25 MINUTES + 2 HOURS OR MORE MARINATING • COOKING: 30 MINUTES

1 tablespoon (15 ml) garlic-ginger paste
(see recipe 6)
3 garlic cloves, chopped
2 green chilies, sliced
1 cup (250 ml) chopped fresh cilantro
1 teaspoon (5 ml) ground cumin

¼ teaspoon (1 ml) garam masala
¼ teaspoon (1 ml) turmeric
1 tablespoon (15 ml) lemon juice
1 tablespoon (15 ml) sunflower oil
1 teaspoon (5 ml) jaggery or soft brown sugar

1 pound (500 g) boneless, skinless chicken
thighs or drumsticks
Sea salt, to taste
7 ounces (200 g) salad leaves
1 cucumber, sliced
Cilantro & mint chutney, to serve

1 2
3 4

1	Blend the garlic-ginger paste, chilies, cilantro, ground spices, lemon juice, oil and jaggery in a food processor or blender and blend until smooth.	2	Put the chicken in a nonmetallic bowl, add the spice mixture, cover and allow to marinate for 2 hours, or longer if time permits.
3	Preheat a grill pan and cook the chicken until tender.	4	Arrange salad leaves on dinner plates, top with the chicken and sliced cucumber and serve with the cilantro & mint chutney (see recipe 71).

SPICY MUSTARD CHICKEN

❧ SERVES 4 • PREPARATION: 30 MINUTES • COOKING: 40 MINUTES ❧

2 tablespoons (30 ml) sunflower oil
1 teaspoon (5 ml) cumin seeds
1 teaspoon (5 ml) black mustard seeds
1 teaspoon (5 ml) fennel seeds
1 teaspoon (5 ml) black onion seeds (nigella)

1 red onion, diced
1 tablespoon (15 ml) garlic-ginger paste
  (see recipe 6)
1 pound (500 g) boneless, skinless chicken
  thighs, cut into bite-sized pieces.

10 ounces (300 g) ripe tomatoes, diced
  (about 1 cup/250 ml)
1 tablespoon (15 ml) tamarind water
1 tablespoon (15 ml) jaggery or soft
  brown sugar

1	Heat the oil in a pan, add the cumin seeds, mustard seeds, fennel seeds and black onion seeds and cook until the mustard seeds pop.	2	Add the onion and garlic-ginger paste and brown lightly.
3	Add the chicken and cook until it changes color. Stir in the tomatoes, tamarind and jaggery or sugar.	4	Bring to a boil, reduce the heat and simmer until the sauce is thick and the chicken is tender. Serve with chapati (see recipe 59).

AWADHI CHICKEN

❧ SERVES 4 • PREPARATION: 15 MINUTES + 2 HOURS OR MORE MARINATING • COOKING: 1 HOUR ❧

2 tablespoons (30 ml) ghee
2 tablespoons (30 ml) sunflower oil
2 onions, sliced
½ cup (125 ml) cashews

1 cinnamon stick
3 whole cloves
3 green cardamom pods, lightly crushed
1 (3-pound/1.3 kg) whole chicken

Generous pinch of saffron threads
1 tablespoon (15 ml) rosewater
½ cup + 2 tablespoons (155 ml) water

1 2
3 4

1	Preheat oven to 400°F (200°C). Heat the ghee and 1 tablespoon (15 ml) oil and fry the onions and cashews until golden.	2	Dry-roast the cinnamon, cloves and cardamom until fragrant, then blend in a food processor or blender to form a powder.
3	Spread the powder over the chicken and marinate for 2 hours, or longer if time permits. Drizzle the remaining oil over top.	4	Meanwhile, put the saffron, rosewater and 2 tablespoons (30 ml) water in a small pot and heat for 3 minutes. ➤

| 5 | Put the chicken in a baking dish with ½ cup (125 ml) water and bake for 50 minutes, until the chicken is golden and tender. Cover and allow to rest for 10 minutes. | **VARIATION**
❁
The chicken can also be cooked in a covered barbecue. This will give it a wonderful smoky flavor that will be delicious with the aromatic spices. |

6	Drizzle the saffron mixture over the chicken and serve.	**TIP** ❂ Rather than cook a whole chicken you can marinate and bake chicken pieces, but remember to adjust the cooking time accordingly.

BUTTER CHICKEN

❖ SERVES 4 • PREPARATION: 20 MINUTES • COOKING: 40 MINUTES ❖

2 pounds (1 kg) boneless, skinless chicken
    thighs, cut into bite-sized pieces
3 tablespoons (45 ml) tandoori masala
1 tablespoon (15 ml) garlic-ginger paste
    (see recipe 6)

½ cup (125 ml) plain yogurt
3 (14-ounce/398 ml) cans diced tomatoes
1 teaspoon (5 ml) garam masala
½ teaspoon (2 ml) paprika
1 cup (250 ml) light cream (20%)

2 tablespoons (30 ml) grated palm sugar or
    soft brown sugar
3 tablespoons (45 ml) chilled ghee
½ teaspoon (2 ml) salt
2 tablespoons (30 ml) chopped fresh cilantro

1 2
3 4

1	Preheat a grill. Put the chicken in a bowl, add the tandoori masala, garlic-ginger paste and yogurt and mix well, until the chicken is coated.	2	Arrange the chicken in a shallow baking dish and cook under the hot grill until tender.	
3	Remove the chicken from the dish and set aside.	4	Pour the juices from the baking dish into a pan and add the tomatoes, garam masala, paprika, cream and sugar.	➤

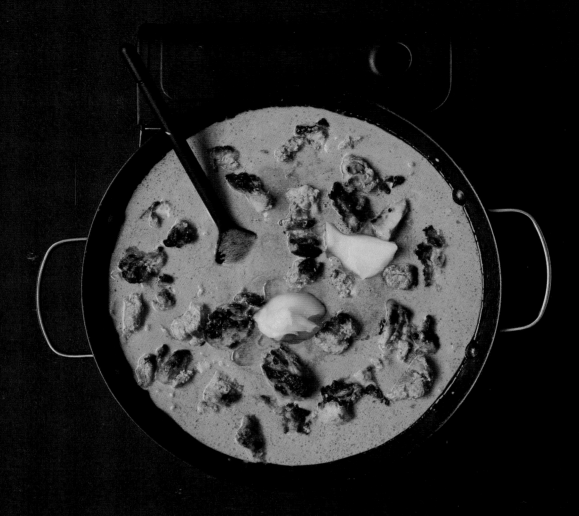

5 | Bring the mixture to a boil and cook over high heat for 10 minutes, until the sauce is thick and creamy. Add the cooked chicken, the ghee and salt and simmer for 3 minutes, until the ghee melts and the chicken is heated through.

NOTE

This dish is very rich, so you may want to leave out the ghee at the end if you would like to reduce the amount of fat.

6	Sprinkle the cilantro on top and serve with lime wedges and freshly cooked rice.	**TIP** ❋ If you marinate the chicken overnight the flavor will be more intense. Make sure you grill the chicken until it blackens slightly, as this adds to the color and the flavor of the final dish.

SEAFOOD FRY

❧ SERVES 4 • PREPARATION: 20 MINUTES • COOKING: 20 MINUTES ❧

1 pound (500 g) raw shrimp
7 ounces (200 g) squid bodies sliced
  into rings
8 ounces (250 g) live mussels
½ teaspoon (2 ml) turmeric
½ teaspoon (2 ml) chili powder

½ teaspoon (2 ml) salt
2 tablespoons (30 ml) garlic-ginger paste
  (see recipe 6)
2 tablespoons (30 ml) sunflower oil
1 tablespoon (15 ml) lemon juice
8 curry leaves

1 teaspoon (5 ml) grated jaggery or soft
  brown sugar
1 tablespoon (15 ml) tamarind water
¼ cup (60 ml) fresh cilantro leaves
Lemon wedges, to serve

| 1 | Peel and devein the shrimp, slice the squid and scrub the mussels. Discard any mussels that are open and that do not close when tapped. | 2 | Put the seafood, turmeric, chili, salt and garlic-ginger paste in a bowl and mix well to coat the seafood. |
| 3 | Heat the oil and stir-fry the seafood. Push it to one side and add the lemon juice, curry leaves, jaggery and tamarind water. | 4 | Discard any mussels that have not opened. Sprinkle the cilantro on top and serve with lemon wedges. |

SHRIMP CURRY

❖ SERVES 4 • PREPARATION: 25 MINUTES • COOKING: 25 MINUTES ❖

1 red onion, chopped
1 tablespoon (15 ml) chopped fresh ginger
2 garlic cloves, chopped
1 green chili, halved and seeded
1 pound (500 g) tomatoes, chopped
   (about 1½ cups/375 ml)

1 teaspoon (5 ml) black mustard seeds
1 teaspoon (5 ml) cumin seeds
1 tablespoon (15 ml) ghee
½ teaspoon (2 ml) turmeric
6 curry leaves
1 tablespoon (15 ml) water

7 fluid ounces (200 ml) coconut milk
2 tablespoons (30 ml) tamarind water
1 tablespoon (15 ml) grated jaggery or
   brown sugar
1½ pounds (750 g) raw shrimp, peeled
   and deveined

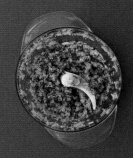

1

2

3

4

5

6 -

1	Blend the onion, ginger, garlic and chili in a food processor or blender until smooth.	2	Clean the appliance then blend the tomatoes until smooth.	3	Fry the seeds in the ghee until they pop. Add the turmeric and curry leaves and fry briefly.
4	Add the onion paste and water and cook for 5 minutes.	5	Add the tomatoes, coconut, milk, tamarind and jaggery and cook until thick.	6	Add the shrimp and cook for 5 minutes, until tender. Serve with rice.

SOUTH INDIAN FRIED SHRIMP

⇥ SERVES 4 • PREPARATION: 25 MINUTES • COOKING: 15 MINUTES ⇤

2 tablespoons (30 ml) ghee
1 pound (500 g) raw shrimp, peeled and
   deveined, tails left intact
2 garlic cloves, chopped
4 small pappadams

Sunflower oil, for frying
1 teaspoon (5 ml) fennel seeds
1 teaspoon (5 ml) brown mustard seeds
Walnut-sized piece of tamarind pulp
½ cup (125 ml) boiling water

2 tomatoes, finely chopped
½ small red onion, finely chopped
½ teaspoon (2 ml) black pepper
2 tablespoons (30 ml) chopped fresh mint
Lemon wedges, to serve

1	Heat half the ghee and stir-fry the shrimp and garlic until the shrimp are pink and tender.	2	Cook the pappadams in hot oil until crisp then drain on paper towels.	3	Heat the remaining ghee and fry the seeds until the mustard seeds pop.
4	Pour the boiling water over the tamarind, stir, strain and press the pulp.	5	Combine the rest of the ingredients, 1 tablespoon (15 ml) of the tamarind water and the fried seeds.	6	Dress the shrimp in the sauce and serve with pappadams, lemon wedges and tomato raita.

GOAN FISH

❖ SERVES 4 • PREPARATION: 15 MINUTES • COOKING: 20 MINUTES ❖

4 small or 1 large flat fish, cleaned
Sunflower oil, for shallow-frying
1 lemon, cut into wedges

SPICE PASTE:
½ teaspoon (2 ml) cumin seeds

½ teaspoon (2 ml) coriander seeds
3 black peppercorns
4 dried red chilies, soaked in hot water and drained
¼ teaspoon (1 ml) turmeric
1 small red onion, chopped

1 tablespoon (15 ml) chopped fresh ginger
6 garlic cloves
1 tablespoon (15 ml) tamarind water
Sea salt, to taste
1 teaspoon (5 ml) sugar
2 tablespoons (30 ml) white vinegar

1	To make the spice paste, dry-roast the cumin, coriander seeds and black peppercorns in a pan until fragrant.	2	Blend the chiles, roasted spices, turmeric, onion, ginger, garlic, tamarind, salt and sugar in a food processor or blender until smooth. Stir in the vinegar.
3	Slice each fish along the top to form a pocket down the center of the fish.	4	Fill the pocket with the spice mix and secure with two toothpicks. ➤

	Heat the oil for shallow-frying and fry the fish until cooked through and crisp and golden brown on both sides.	**VARIATION** ❁
5		If you can't find a flat fish, you can use a large fish instead. To make the pocket to stuff, cut behind the head, down the spine and to the tail on both sides.

	Drain the fish on paper towels and serve with salad and the lemon wedges.	**TIP** Make sure the fish is dry before putting it in the hot oil. Rub both sides with a little oil, as this will help to stop it from sticking to the bottom of the pan.
6		

FISH MOLEE

❖ SERVES 4 • PREPARATION: 25 MINUTES • COOKING: 40 MINUTES ❖

2 tablespoons (30 ml) sunflower oil
1 teaspoon (5 ml) black mustard seeds
½ teaspoon (2 ml) fenugreek seeds
10 curry leaves
2 green chilies, split lengthways

1 red onion, sliced
1 tablespoon (15 ml) tamarind concentrate
½ teaspoon (2 ml) turmeric
½ teaspoon (2 ml) salt
½ teaspoon (2 ml) cracked black pepper

1½ cups (375 ml) coconut milk
1 pound (500 g) boneless firm white fish
    fillets (e.g., snapper, cod), cut into chunks
1 medium tomato, chopped

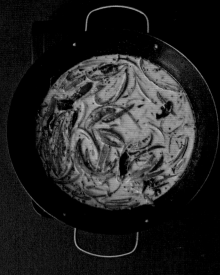

1 2
3 4

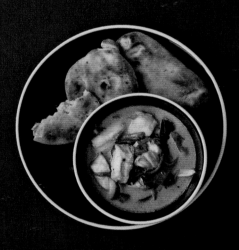

1	Heat the oil and fry the mustard and fenugreek seeds until they pop. Add the curry leaves, chilies and onion and cook for 10 minutes.	2	Add the tamarind, turmeric, salt, pepper and half of the coconut milk. Bring to a boil.
3	Reduce the heat, add the fish and simmer for 5–10 minutes, turning the fish a couple of times during cooking.	4	Add the remaining coconut milk and the tomatoes and simmer for 10 minutes, until the oil rises to the surface of the curry. Serve with naan bread (see recipe 62).

BENGALI FISH ROLLS

MAKES 12 • PREPARATION: 40 MINUTES + 1–2 HOURS CHILLING • COOKING: 20 MINUTES

1 pound (500 g) boneless firm, white
    fish fillets
2 large potatoes
1 green chilies, chopped (optional)
1 tablespoon (15 ml) chopped fresh cilantro

½ teaspoon (2 ml) ground cinnamon
1 egg white, lightly beaten
Sea salt
Black pepper, to taste
1 cup (250 ml) fresh breadcrumbs

Sunflower oil, for shallow-frying
Lemon wedges, to serve

1 2
3 4

1	Steam the fish fillets and potatoes until tender. Allow to cool slightly. Flake the fish with a fork, mash the potatoes and combine in a bowl.	2	Add the chili, if using, cilantro, cinnamon, egg white, salt and pepper to the fish and potato mixture, and combine.
3	Shape 2–3 tablespoons (30–45 ml) of the mixture into small sausage shapes. Roll in the breadcrumbs. Chill for 1–2 hours, until firm.	4	Heat the oil for shallow-frying and fry the rolls until crisp and golden. Serve with lemon wedges.

GRILLED FISH IN BANANA LEAF

❧ MAKES 4 • PREPARATION: 20 MINUTES • COOKING: 30 MINUTES ❧

½ teaspoon (2 ml) turmeric
1 teaspoon (5 ml) cracked black pepper
1 teaspoon (5 ml) salt
4 salmon fillets, skin on
Sunflower oil, for shallow-frying

1 red onion
1 green chili, seeded
⅓ cup (75 ml) chopped fresh cilantro
4 garlic cloves

1¼-inch (3 cm) piece fresh ginger, peeled
   and chopped
Young banana leaves
Lime wedges, to serve

1 2
3 4

1	Preheat oven to 425°F (220°C). Combine the turmeric, pepper and salt and rub into the fish. Heat the oil and fry the fish.	2	Remove the fish and all but 3 tablespoons (45 ml) oil. Blend the onion, chili, cilantro, garlic and ginger in a food processor or blender until smooth.	
3	Heat the remaining 3 tablespoons (45 ml) oil and cook the onion-cilantro paste for 15 minutes, until caramelized.	4	Heat the banana leaves over an open gas flame or under a hot grill until they are soft and pliable.	➤

| 5 | Spread the paste on top of the fish, then wrap the fish in the softened banana leaves and secure with string. | **NOTE**
❋
You can use foil or parchment paper instead of the banana leaves. You can also prepare the salmon parcels ahead of time and cook them just before serving. Make sure you bring them up to room temperature by taking them out of the refrigerator 30 minutes before baking. |

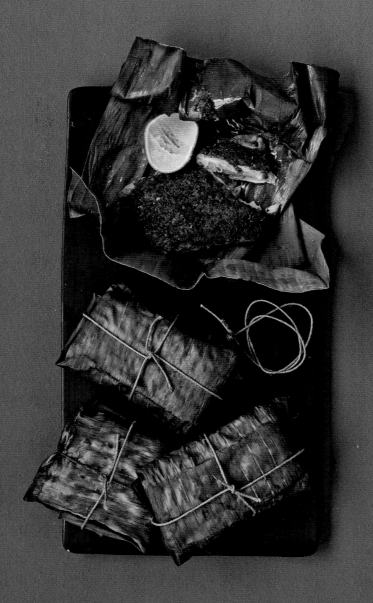

6	Put the salmon parcels on a nonstick baking sheet and bake for 10–15 minutes, until the fish is tender. Serve with lime wedges.	**TIP** ※ These parcels make an excellent dish for a dinner party. Take the parcels to the table and let guests unwrap them. The banana leaves can also act as plates.

BATTERED FISH

❖ SERVES 4 • PREPARATION: 25 MINUTES • COOKING: 30 MINUTES ❖

1 cup (250 ml) chickpea flour (besan)
1 teaspoon (5 ml) ground cumin
½ teaspoon (2 ml) ground coriander
2 teaspoons (10 ml) chaat masala

¼ teaspoon (1 ml) cracked black pepper
2 tablespoons (30 ml) chopped fresh cilantro
½ cup (125 ml) soda water or beer
4 pieces boneless white fish fillets, cut into
   long, thin strips

Sunflower oil, for deep-frying
Lemon wedges, to serve

1	Combine the flour, spices, cilantro and soda water or beer to form a smooth batter. Allow to stand for 10 minutes.	2	Dip the fish into the batter, allowing any excess to drip off.
3	Heat the oil for deep-frying and fry the fish until crisp and golden.	4	Drain on paper towls. Serve with lemon wedges.

BREADS & RICE

5

BREADS

RICE

CHAPATI

❧ MAKES 8 • PREPARATION: 30 MINUTES • COOKING: 10 MINUTES ❧

Ayurvedic

1½ cups (375 ml) atta or whole wheat flour
Pinch of salt, to taste
½ cup (125 ml) water
3 tablespoons (45 ml) ghee

1	Put the flour and salt in a bowl.	2	Add the water and mix until the dough starts to stick together.
3	Continue adding water 1 tablespoon (15 ml) at a time until the dough forms into a ball.	4	Knead the dough until smooth. It will spring back when you touch it. ➤

5 6
7 8

5	Break off 1 tablespoon (15 ml) of dough and roll it out to form a circle, dipping it in flour a couple of times to stop it from sticking to the pan.	6	Heat a tawa or roti pan or a nonstick frying pan and cook one of the dough circles on one side until bubbles appear.
7	Turn the chapati over and pat it down with a clean paper towel until it puffs and rises.	8	Brush the chapati with ghee.

9 Wrap the chapatis in a clean dish towel and keep them warm while you roll out and cook the remaining dough. Serve as part of any Indian meal.

TIP
❋

Make sure you add the water gradually when you are making the dough: sticky dough will lead to heavy chapatis. Do not turn the chapatis over when rolling them out, and keep them well floured. A chapati roller will help you to roll them out into a circle.

POORI

❧ MAKES 14 • PREPARATION: 30 MINUTES • COOKING: 20 MINUTES ❧

1 cup (250 ml) maida or all-purpose flour
1 cup (250 ml) atta or whole wheat flour
1 tablespoon (15 ml) ghee

Pinch of salt
½ cup (125 ml) water
Sunflower oil, for deep-frying

1 2
3 4

1	Put the flours in a bowl, cut in the ghee and add the salt.	2	Add nearly all of the water and mix until the dough sticks together. Add the rest of the water 1 tablespoon (15 ml) at a time, until the dough forms a ball.
3	Knead the dough until smooth. It will spring back when you touch it. Break off 1 tablespoon (15 ml) of the dough and roll into a ball.	4	Dip the dough into oil and roll out from the center, turning as you roll to form a circle. Do not turn the dough over. ➤

5	Heat the oil for deep-frying in a large pot. Drop a dough circle into the hot oil, and ladle the hot oil over it when it rises to the surface. Press the circle down with the back of the spoon to ensure it stays submerged in the oil.	**VARIATION** ❋ You can add beet juice or spinach juice to the dough to change its color.

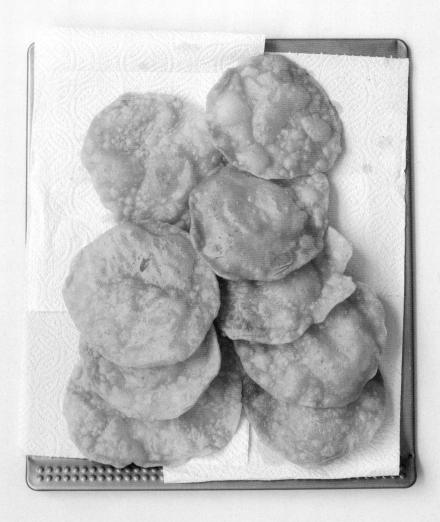

| 6 | Turn the poori over and cook until crisp and golden. Drain on paper towels and serve immediately. | **NOTE**
❋
Poori are rolled out on an oiled surface, not a floured one. Cook the poori one at a time so you can focus on the job at hand. Gently spoon the hot oil over the poori. Keep it submerged in the hot oil once it starts to puff up. |

STUFFED PARATHA

❧ MAKES 8 • PREPARATION: 25 MINUTES • COOKING: 20 MINUTES ❧

Ayurvedic

FILLING:
1 medium potato (about 5 ounces/150 g), unpeeled
1 small onion, grated
½ cup (125 ml) finely shredded spinach

1 teaspoon (5 ml) grated fresh ginger
½ teaspoon (2 ml) ajowan seeds
½ teaspoon (2 ml) turmeric
1 tablespoon (15 ml) chopped fresh cilantro

PARATHA:
2 cups (500 ml) atta or whole wheat flour
Pinch of salt
2 teaspoons (10 ml) ghee
½ cup (125 ml) water

1	To make the filling, steam the potato then allow to cool slightly, peel and mash.	2	Add the onion, spinach, ginger, ajowan seeds, turmeric and cilantro to the potatoes and combine.
3	Combine flour, salt and ghee. Mix in most of the water. Add the remaining water 1 tablespoon (15 ml) at a time, until the dough forms a ball.	4	Knead the dough until smooth. It will spring back when you touch it. Divide the dough into 12 portions. ➤

| 5 | Roll out one ball of dough on a lightly floured surface until it is smooth and round. Spread 1–2 tablespoons (15–30 ml) of the filling over the circle, leaving an edge of about ¾ inch (2 cm) — this will stop the filling from oozing out. Roll another ball into a circle and place it on top of the first circle. Press the edges to seal. |

VARIATION
❋

Parathas can be filled with various fillings, such as herbs, spinach or spices. Parathas can also be cooked plain, without any filling.

	Heat a tawa or roti pan or a nonstick frying pan, add a paratha and cook, turning over once, until both sides are golden brown. Repeat with the remaining dough. Keep the parathas in a warm oven while you cook the rest.	**NOTE** ❋ Make parathas ahead of time and reheat them in a warm oven. They are best kept warm in a clean paper towel.
6		

NAAN

❧ MAKES 6 • PREPARATION: 30 MINUTES + 3–4 HOURS RISING • COOKING: 20 MINUTES ❧

¾ cup (175 ml) lukewarm water
1 teaspoon (5 ml) superfine sugar
1 teaspoon (5 ml) active dry yeast
2 cups (500 ml) maida or all-purpose flour

1 teaspoon (5 ml) baking powder
Pinch of salt
2½ tablespoons (37 ml) plain yogurt
2 tablespoons (30 ml) sunflower oil

3 tablepoons (45 ml) ghee
3 garlic cloves, chopped

1 2
3 4

1	Preheat oven to 500°F (260°C). Combine the water, sugar and yeast and let stand until foamy.	2	Combine the flour, baking powder and salt in a bowl.
3	Gradually add the yeast mixture and yogurt to the dry ingredients and mix until the dough comes together.	4	Knead for a few minutes, until smooth. ➤

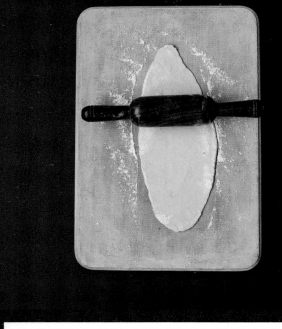

5	Cover and set aside for 3–4 hours, until the dough doubles in size.	6	Using lightly oiled hands, divide the dough into 6 balls.
7	Roll out each dough ball on a lightly floured surface, creating a large oblong shape.	8	Place the dough oblongs on a pizza stone or baking sheet and bake for 3 minutes, until puffed and golden.

| 9 | Melt the ghee and lightly fry the garlic. Brush the ghee-garlic mixture onto the naan. Serve warm. | **TIP** ✳ You can fill the center of each dough ball with a combination of grated paneer, chopped almonds and raisins to make stuffed naan. |

SAFFRON RICE

❧ SERVES 4 • PREPARATION: 20 MINUTES • COOKING: 25 MINUTES ❧

1½ cups (375 ml) basmati rice
1 tablespoon (15 ml) sunflower oil
3 tablespoons (45 ml) ghee
2 onions, sliced
¼ teaspoon (1 ml) turmeric
1 teaspoon (5 ml) cumin seeds

2 brown cardamom pods, lightly crushed
1 cinnamon stick
1 bay leaf
Generous pinch of saffron threads
2 cups (500 ml) water

VARIATION:
Make delicous coconut rice by substituting 1 cup (250 ml) coconut milk for half the water.

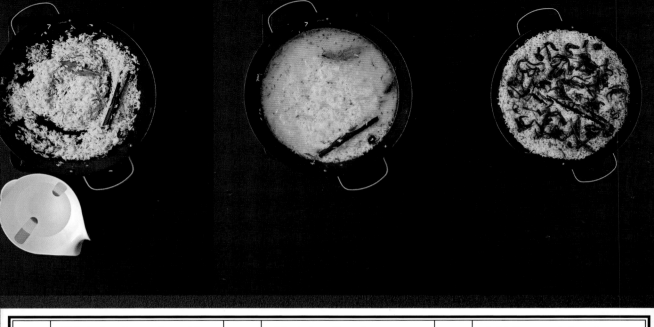

1	Wash the rice under cold running water until the water runs clear.	2	Heat the oil and 2 tablespoons (30 ml) ghee and brown the onions. Remove from the pan.	3	Add the remaining ghee and spices and cook for 2 minutes, until fragrant.
4	Stir in the rice and the water, and bring to a boil.	5	Cover and cook for 15 minutes, or until the rice is tender.	6	Serve the rice topped with the caramelized onions.

KHICHDI

❖ SERVES 4 • PREPARATION: 15 MINUTES • COOKING: 50 MINUTES ❖

1 tablespoon (15 ml) ghee	Sea salt, to taste	½ cup (125 ml) split mung beans, with husks
½ teaspoon (2 ml) fennel seeds	1 small red onion, finely chopped	6 cups (1.5 L) water
1 teaspoon (5 ml) cumin seeds	1 teaspoon (5 ml) grated fresh ginger	2 tablespoons (30 ml) chopped fresh cilantro
¼ teaspoon (1 ml) turmeric	1 cup (250 ml) basmati rice	Lemon juice, to taste

1	Heat the ghee in a pot, add the fennel, cumin, turmeric and salt and cook until fragrant.	2	Add the onion and ginger and cook until the onion is golden brown.
3	Add the rice, beans and water and bring to a boil. Cook for 40 minutes, until the rice and beans are soft and creamy.	4	Stir the cilantro and lemon juice through the rice, taste, adjust seasoning as needed and serve.

VEGETABLE PILAF

❖ SERVES 4 • PREPARATION: 20 MINUTES • COOKING: 40 MINUTES ❖

3 tablespoons (45 ml) ghee
1 onion, finely chopped
1–2 tablespoons (15–30 ml) garlic-ginger
   paste (see recipe 6)
1 green chili, chopped
1 teaspoon (5 ml) cumin seeds
½ teaspoon (2 ml) turmeric

1 teaspoon (5 ml) garam masala
2 tomatoes, chopped
3½ ounces (100 g) green beans
   (about ¾ cup/175 ml) thinly sliced
1 carrot, diced
3½ ounces (100 g) cauliflower, cut
   into florets

1 cup (250 ml) peas
1½ cups (375 ml) basmati rice
2½ cups (600 ml) water
Sea salt, to taste
2 tablespoons (30 ml) roughly chopped
   cilantro

1	Heat 2 tablespoons (30 ml) ghee in a large, deep frying pan, add the onion and garlic-ginger paste and brown.	2	Add the chili, cumin, turmeric, garam masala and tomatoes and cook until the tomatoes soften.
3	Add the vegetables, rice, water, salt and the remaining ghee and bring to a boil.	4	Cover and cook for 15 minutes, until the rice is soft. Fork the cilantro through the rice and serve.

LAMB BIRYANI

❖ SERVES 4 • PREPARATION: 30 MINUTES + OVERNIGHT MARINATING • COOKING: 40 MINUTES ❖

1 pound (500 g) cubed leg of lamb
2 teaspoons (10 ml) garam masala
¼ teaspoon (1 ml) black pepper
½ teaspoon (2 ml) turmeric
1 green chili, halved

3 tablespoons (45 ml) garlic-ginger paste
   (see recipe 6)
1 cup (250 ml) plain yogurt
3 tablespoons (45 ml) sunflower oil
2 onions, sliced

1½ cups (375 ml) basmati rice
2 tablespoons (30 ml) ghee, melted
Pinch of saffron threads
¼ cup (60 ml) sliced almonds, toasted
2 tablespoons (30 ml) raisins

1	Put the lamb, garam masala, black pepper, turmeric, chile, garlic-ginger paste and yogurt in a bowl and mix until the lamb is coated. Marinate overnight.	2	Preheat oven to 350°F (180°C). Heat the oil and brown the onions. Remove a third of the onions from the pan and set aside for the garnish.	
3	Add the lamb to the pan along with the water and bring to a boil. Reduce heat and cover and cook for 1 hour, until the lamb is tender.	4	In a different pot, cook the rice in enough water to cover it, until it is tender.	➤

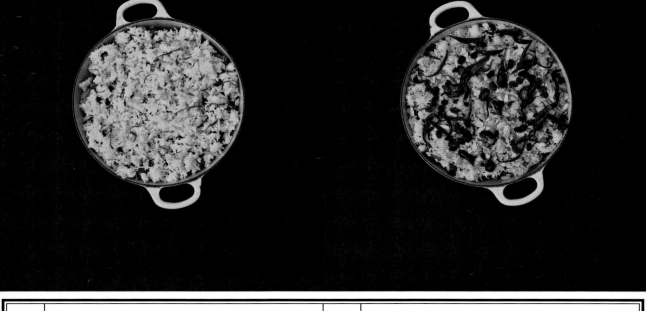

5	Grease a large casserole dish with a little ghee and add half of the rice to the dish.	6	Top with the lamb and then add another layer of rice.
7	Soak the saffron in 1 tablespoon (15 ml) hot water, then drizzle over the rice along with the rest of the ghee. Cover and bake for 30 minutes.	8	Sprinkle with the reserved onions, the almonds and the raisins.

9   Serve hot with chutneys (see recipes 67 to 72), and raitas (see recipe 73) or other condiments.

NOTE
❋

This recipe is best served and eaten right after it has been cooked. Team it with yogurt or raita and serve with lemon wedges. It is a wonderful dish for special occasions as it looks really impressive.

CHUTNEYS, PICKLES & SALADS

6

CHUTNEYS & RAITAS

PICKLES

SALADS

COCONUT CHUTNEY

❧ MAKES ½ CUP (125 ML) • PREPARATION: 5 MINUTES • COOKING: 10 MINUTES ❧

½ cup (125 ml) shredded coconut
1 tablespoon (15 ml) grated fresh ginger
2 tablespoons (30 ml) water
1 tablespoon (15 ml) sunflower oil

1 teaspoon (5 ml) black mustard seeds
1 dried red chili
4 curry leaves
Sea salt, to taste

1 2
3 4

1	Blend the coconut and ginger with the water in a food processor or blender to form a paste. Transfer to a bowl.	2	Heat the oil in a small frying pan and fry the mustard seeds, red chili and curry leaves until the mustard seeds pop.
3	Stir the spiced oil into the coconut mixture, then season to taste with salt.	4	Serve as a condiment with chapati (see recipe 59) or samosas, or as a dip with pappadams (see recipe 8).

TAMARIND CHUTNEY

❧ MAKES 1½ CUPS (375 ML) • PREPARATION: 15 MINUTES • COOKING: 15 MINUTES ❧

2 tablespoons (30 ml) sunflower oil
1 teaspoon (5 ml) cumin seeds
1 teaspoon (5 ml) coriander seeds
¼ teaspoon (1 ml) chili powder (optional)

½ cup (125 ml) grated jaggery or soft
   brown sugar
1 tablespoon (15 ml) water
1 cup (250 ml) tamarind water

½ teaspoon (2 ml) dried ground ginger
½ teaspoon (2 ml) sea salt

1	Heat the oil in a pot and fry the cumin seeds, coriander seeds and chili powder until the spices are fragrant.	2	Add the jaggery and water and cook, stirring, until the sugar has dissolved.
3	Stir in the tamarind water and ginger then boil for 10 minutes, until the mixture is reduced by a third and thickened slightly.	4	Stir in the salt then spoon into a sterilized jar and seal. It will keep for 3 months. Serve with chaat (see recipe 77) or samosas (see recipe 12).

TOMATO CHUTNEY

❧ MAKES 5 CUPS (1.25 L) • PREPARATION: 20 MINUTES • COOKING: 40 MINUTES ❧

1 tablespoon (15 ml) sunflower oil
1 teaspoon (5 ml) black mustard seeds
1 teaspoon (5 ml) cumin seeds
1 teaspoon (5 ml) fenugreek seeds
1 teaspoon (5 ml) fennel seeds

2 pounds (1 kg) ripe tomatoes, chopped
  (about 1½ cups/375 ml)
½ cup (125 ml) raisins
1 cup (250 ml) grated jaggery or soft
  brown sugar

1 cup (250 ml) chopped pitted dates
2 tablespoons (30 ml) white vinegar
1 teaspoon (5 ml) salt

1 2
3 4

1	Heat the oil and fry the mustard, cumin, fenugreek and fennel seeds until the mustard seeeds pop.	2	Add the tomatoes and cook until they begin to soften.
3	Add the raisins, jaggery, dates, vinegar and salt and simmer for about 20 minutes, until the mixture is thick and pulpy.	4	Spoon into sterilized jars and seal. Serve with samosas (see recipe 12) and egg chapati (see recipe 13).

MANGO CHUTNEY

❧ SERVES 4 • PREPARATION: 15 MINUTES • COOKING: 45 MINUTES ❧

5 pounds (2.5 kg) underripe mangoes
1 red onion, chopped
1 tablespoon (15 ml) grated fresh ginger
½ cup + 2 tablespoons (155 ml) white
  vinegar

½ cup (125 ml) grated jaggery or grated
  palm sugar
½ teaspoon (2 ml) garam masala
¼ teaspoon (1 ml) ground cardamom
½ teaspoon (2 ml) chili powder

1	Peel the mangoes, remove the pits and chop the flesh.	2	Cook the mango, onion, ginger, vinegar, jaggery, garam masala, cardamom and chili over a low heat until the sugar has dissolved.
3	Bring to a boil, reduce heat and simmer for about 40 minutes. Check often to ensure mixture is not sticking to the bottom of the pot.	4	Spoon the mixture into warm, dry jars, pushing down to remove any air. Seal with vinegar-proof lids. Store for a few months before eating.

CILANTRO & MINT CHUTNEY

✣ MAKES ½ CUP (125 ML) • PREPARATION: 10 MINUTES • COOKING: NONE ✣

2 green chilies
½ cup (125 ml) fresh mint leaves
1 cup (250 ml) fresh cilantro leaves
1 garlic clove, chopped

1 small red onion, chopped
1 tablespoon (15 ml) lemon juice
1 teaspoon (5 ml) sugar
Sea salt, to taste

1 2
3 4

1	Cut the chilies in half and remove the seeds and membrane with a spoon, discard, then chop the chili flesh. Put the chilies in a food processor or blender.	2	Add the mint, cilantro, garlic, onion, lemon juice, sugar, salt and 2 tablespoons (30 ml) water and blend until smooth.
3	If using the chutney for sandwiches leave at this consistency; if using it for chaats add 1–2 tablespoons (15–30 ml) water and blend.	4	Serve with breads and dosa or with snacks, such as samosas (see recipe 12).

CILANTRO YOGURT CHUTNEY

⇢ MAKES ¾ CUP (175 ML) • PREPARATION: 10 MINUTES • COOKING: NONE ⇠

2 garlic cloves
Fresh root ginger, to taste
2 lemons
½ cup (125 ml) fresh mint leaves

1 cup (250 ml) fresh cilantro leaves
1 teaspoon (5 ml) sugar
Sea salt, to taste
¾ cup (175 ml) plain yogurt

1	Chop the garlic, peel the ginger then grate it, and juice the lemons.	2	Put the garlic, ginger, lemon juice, mint, cilantro, sugar, salt and yogurt in a food processor or blender.
3	Process until the mixture is smooth.	4	Serve as a dip with pappadams (see recipe 8) or use as a dressing for kebabs.

RAITAS

❧ SERVES 4 • PREPARATION: 10 MINUTES • COOKING: NONE ❧

CACHUMBER
Put 2 diced tomatoes and 1 diced small red onion in a bowl. Add 1 tablespoon (15 ml) chopped fresh cilantro, 2 teaspoons (5 ml) lemon juice and 1 pinch salt. Mix.

CUCUMBER RAITA
Put ½ diced cucumber in a bowl. Add ½ cup (125 ml) plain yogurt, ¼ teaspoon (2 ml) cumin, ¼ teaspoon (2 ml) salt, ¼ teaspoon (2 ml) sugar and 1 tablespoon (15 ml) chopped fresh cilantro and mint. Mix.

RAITAS

❧ SERVES 4 • PREPARATION: 10 MINUTES • COOKING: NONE ❧

BANANA RAITA

Put 3 thickly sliced bananas in a bowl. Drizzle over 1 tablespoon (15 ml) lemon juice and combine. Fold through ¼ cup (60 ml) shredded coconut, 1 tablespoon (15 ml) chopped fresh cilantro and season to taste with salt.

POMEGRANATE RAITA

Put ½ cup (125 ml) plain yogurt into a bowl, add ¼ cup (60 ml) pomegranate seeds, ¼ cup (60 ml) roughly chopped fresh mint leaves, ½ teaspoon (2 ml) ground cumin and combine well.

LIME PICKLE

❧ MAKES 8 CUPS (2 L) • PREPARATION: 30 MINUTES + 2 WEEKS STANDING • COOKING: 5 MINUTES ☙

16 limes
1 cup (250 ml) salt
1 teaspoon (5 ml) fenugreek seeds
1 teaspoon (5 ml) black mustard seeds
2 tablespoons (30 ml) sunflower oil

2 teaspoons (10 ml) turmeric
1 teaspoon (5 ml) asafetida
½ cup (125 ml) chili powder
2 tablespoons (30 ml) superfine sugar

NOTE:
Store for 2 weeks at room temperature in a sunny place to pickle. The pickles can be stored in the refrigerator for up to 6 months.

1 2
3 4

1	Wash and dry the limes. Cut each in half, then into quarters, then cut each quarter in half. Put into a bowl, add the salt and mix.	2	Pack the limes into a clean, dry 4-cup (1 L) glass jar. Seal and allow to stand at room temperature for 1 week.
3	Fry the seeds in hot oil for 1 minute. Put in a mortar, add the turmeric and asafetida and grind with a pestle to form a powder.	4	Put the spice mixture, chili powder, sugar and limes into a clean, dry nonmetallic bowl and mix. Spoon the mixture into the jar and seal.

EGGPLANT PICKLE

➤ MAKES 3⅔ CUPS (900 ML) • PREPARATION: 30 MINUTES + 30 MINUTES STANDING • COOKING: 35 MINUTES ➤

2 large eggplants
3 tablespoons (45 ml) salt
1 teaspoon (5 ml) turmeric
2 teaspoons (10 ml) chili powder

1 teaspoon (5 ml) ground cumin
1 teaspoon (5 ml) fenugreek seeds
1 cup (250 ml) sunflower oil
3 tablespoons (45 ml) garlic-ginger paste
(see recipe 6)

2 small green chilies
6 curry leaves
1 cup (250 ml) malt vinegar
2 tablespoons (30 ml) jaggery or soft
brown sugar

1 2
3 4

1	Cut the eggplants into cubes, place in a colander and sprinkle with salt. Allow to stand for 30 minutes.	2	Fry the turmeric, chili powder, cumin and fenugreek in oil for 5 minutes. Add the paste, chilies and curry leaves and cook for 10 minutes.
3	Add the eggplant, vinegar and jaggery and cook for 15–20 minutes, until the eggplant is soft.	4	Spoon into warm, dry jars, pushing down to remove any air. Seal with vinegar-proof lids. Store for a few weeks before eating.

CABBAGE SALAD

❧ SERVES 4 • PREPARATION: 10 MINUTES • COOKING: 10 MINUTES ❧

Ayurvedic

1½ tablespoons (22 ml) sunflower oil
1 teaspoon (5 ml) black mustard seeds
1 teaspoon (5 ml) asafetida
6 curry leaves
2 green chilies, halved

2 tablespoons (30 ml) lemon juice
4 cups (1 L) chopped cabbage
1 carrot, grated
⅔ cup (150 g) almonds, chopped

Sea salt, to taste
Lemon wedges, to serve

1 2
3 4

1	Heat the oil and fry the mustard seeds until they pop. Add the asafetida.	2	Add the curry leaves, chilies and lemon juice.
3	Add the cabbage, carrot and almonds. Season with salt.	4	Toss and cook until heated through. Serve at room temperature with lemon wedges.

FRUIT CHAAT

❖ SERVES 4 • PREPARATION: 10 MINUTES • COOKING: NONE ❖

2 pomegranates
2 apples, cored and chopped into bite-sized
  pieces
2 bananas, sliced
2 mandarins, peeled and segmented
1 papaya, chopped

2 tablespoons (30 ml) lemon juice
½ teaspoon (2 ml) chaat masala

NOTE:
This is a great way to get children or fussy
eaters to eat more fruit. The chaat masala

adds a little zing and spice to the fruit,
making it irresistible. If you are unable to
find chaat masala you can use a little black
Indian salt and some freshly ground cumin
instead. The spices also make the fruit
more digestible.

1 2
3 4

1	Cut the pomegranates in half, place over a bowl and tap the top of the fruit with a spoon to release the seeds.	2	Put all the fruits into a nonmetallic bowl and combine.
3	Add the lemon juice and chaat masala.	4	Mix well to coat the fruit in the spice mixture. Serve for breakfast with yogurt or as a snack.

DESSERTS & DRINKS

7

DESSERTS

DRINKS

CARROT HALVAH

❖ SERVES 4–6 • PREPARATION: 20 MINUTES • COOKING: 40 MINUTES ❖

Ayurvedic

4 cardamom pods
2 tablespoons (30 ml) ghee
4 carrots, grated
⅓ cup (75 ml) raw almonds, roughly
   chopped

2 cups (500 ml) unhomogenized milk
Scant ½ cup (100 ml) shelled pistachios,
   roughly chopped
1 cup (250 ml) soft brown sugar
Pinch of ground cardamom, for sprinkling

TIP:
You can substitute butter for the ghee, using
exactly the same quantity. However, the halvah will no longer be Ayurvedic, as butter
has different properties to ghee and doesn't
have the medicinal qualities.

1	Lightly crush the cardamom pods using a mortar and pestle.	2	Heat the ghee and cook the carrots for 5 minutes, until they start to soften.	3	Add the milk, half the almonds and the cardamom pods.
4	Cook, stirring occasionally, until the milk has been absorbed by the carrots.	5	Add the sugar and stir to combine.	6	Serve with the reserved nuts and a sprinkling of ground cardamom.

MUNG BEAN PANCAKES

✈ SERVES 6 • PREPARATION: 15 MINUTES • COOKING: 40 MINUTES ✦

¼ cup (60 ml) split mung beans, husked
2 cups (500 ml) water
1 cup (250 ml) atta or whole wheat flour
1 teaspoon (5 ml) baking powder
¼ cup (60 ml) grated jaggery or soft
   brown sugar

½ cup (125 ml) milk
⅓ cup (75 ml) ghee

JAGGERY SYRUP:
1 tablespoon (15 ml) grated fresh ginger
6 green cardamom pods, lightly crushed

1 teaspoon (5 ml) ground cumin
¼ teaspoon (1 ml) crushed black pepper
½ cup (125 ml) grated jaggery or soft
   brown sugar
1 cup (250 ml) water

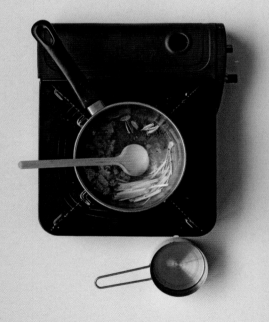

1	Put the beans in a pot, cover with the water, bring to a boil and cook for 20 minutes, until the beans are very soft. Set aside to cool.	2	Sift the flour and baking powder into a bowl. Make a well in the center.
3	Add the beans, jaggery, milk and half the ghee and mix to form a smooth batter. Set aside while you make the syrup.	4	Stir syrup ingredients over low heat until jaggery dissolves. Add the water and boil until reduced by half. ➤

5	Heat a little of the remaining ghee in a pan, add ¼ cup (60 ml) of the batter to the pan and cook until bubbles appear on the surface. Flip and cook the other side.	**NOTES** ❊ This batter thickens on standing, so if it looks a little thin set it aside for about 15 minutes to thicken. You can substitute butter for the ghee, using exactly the same quantity. However, the pancakes will no longer be Ayurvedic in nature, as butter has different properties to ghee and doesn't have the same medicinal qualities.

6	You can serve stacks of the pancakes drizzled with jaggery syrup and yogurt.	**TIP** ❋
		The pancakes can be made ahead of time and re-heated, covered, in a moderate oven, 375°F (190°C). The syrup thickens as it cools, so you may need to add a splash of water to it and reheat it gently before serving.

PISTACHIO & MANGO KULFI

Ayurvedic

❧ SERVES 4 • PREPARATION: 30 MINUTES + COOLING AND OVERNIGHT FREEZING • COOKING: 10 MINUTES ❧

1 mango
6 green cardamom pods
1¾ cups (425 ml) evaporated milk

⅔ cup (150 ml) light cream (20%)
2 tablespoons (30 ml) raw sugar
1½ tablespoons (22 ml) ground almonds

1 tablespoon (15 ml) shredded coconut
¼ cup (60 ml) shelled pistachios,
    roughly chopped

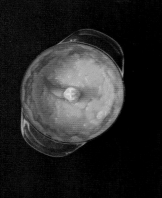

1 2
3 4

1	Remove the flesh from the mangoes, place in a blender or food processor and blend until smooth.	2	Remove the seeds from the cardamom pods and grind with a mortar and pestle to form a fine powder.	
3	Put the milk, cream and sugar in a pot, and stir over low heat until the sugar dissolves. Bring to a boil and cook, stirring, for 5 minutes.	4	Add the almonds, coconut and mango puree and combine. Set aside and allow to cool.	➤

5	Stir in the pistachios. Pour into molds and freeze overnight, until firm.	**NOTE** ※ If the kulfi seems stuck in its mold, run a flat-bladed knife around the edge and gently tap the inverted mold onto a board to break the seal.

	Rub the molds with a damp cloth to release the kulfi. Serve on plates and sprinkle with some pistachios.	**TIP**
6		If serving the kulfi at a dinner party, you can unmold the kulfis before your guests arrive and then return them to the freezer. Try decorating them with edible silver leaf, available at Indian food stores, for special occasions.

SPICED ALMOND COOKIES

➤ MAKES 16 • PREPARATION: 20 MINUTES • COOKING: 25 MINUTES ◄

1 cup (250 ml) all-purpose flour
1 teaspoon (5 ml) ground ginger
½ teaspoon (2 ml) ground cardamom
½ teaspoon (2 ml) ground cinnamon
1 teaspoon (5 ml) baking soda

2 tablespoons (30 ml) ground almonds
Scant ½ cup (100 ml) shelled pistachios
1 cup (250 ml) finely grated jaggery or soft
   brown sugar
½ cup (250 ml) ghee, melted

TIP:
You can substitute butter for the ghee, using exactly the same quantity. However, the cookies will no longer be Ayurvedic, as butter has different properties to ghee and doesn't have the same medicinal qualities.

1	Preheat oven to 315°F (160°C). Sift the flour, ginger, cardamom, cinnamon and baking soda into a bowl.	2	Chop half of the pistachios. Stir in the ground almonds, the chopped pistachios, the jaggery and enough melted ghee to form a dough.
3	Roll heaped teaspoons of the dough into balls and flatten slightly. Top with the remaining whole pistachios.	4	Place on a cookie sheet lined with parchment paper and bake for 20–25 minutes, until crisp and golden. Allow to cool before serving.

VERMICELLI PUDDING

✦ SERVES 4 • PREPARATION: 15 MINUTES • COOKING: 20 MINUTES ✦

Ayurvedic

1 tablespoon (15 ml) ghee
2 green cardamom pods, lightly crushed
1 cup (250 ml) broken vermicelli
3 cups (750 ml) unhomogenized milk
Pinch of saffron threads
Pinch of turmeric

2 tbsp (30 ml) sliced almonds, toasted
2 tbsp (30 ml) pumpkin seeds, toasted
¼ cup (60 ml) raisins
2 tablespoons (30 ml) raw sugar, jaggery or
    soft brown sugar

TIP:
You can substitute butter for the ghee, using exactly the same quantity. However, the pudding will no longer be Ayurvedic, as butter has different properties to ghee and doesn't have the same medicinal qualities.

1	Heat the ghee in a frying pan and cook the cardamom and vermicelli until the vermicelli is golden brown.	2	Put the milk, saffron and turmeric in a pot and slowly bring to a boil.
3	Add the vermicelli, 1 tablespoon (15 ml) each of the almonds and the pumpkin seeds, all of the raisins and the sugar, and cook for 5–10 minutes.	4	Serve the pudding in bowls and sprinkle with a few extra sliced almonds and pumpkin seeds.

CHEWY SPICED YOGURT CAKE

❖ SERVES 8–12 • PREPARATION: 20 MINUTES • COOKING: 1 HOUR 5 MINUTES ❖

3 eggs
1¼ cups (310 ml) brown sugar
⅔ cup (150 ml) ghee
1 cup (250 ml) plain yogurt
1½ cups (375 ml) all-purpose flour
1 teaspoon (5 ml) baking powder

½ teaspoon (2 ml) baking soda
¼ teaspoon (1 ml) salt
1 teaspoon (5 ml) ground cinnamon
½ teaspoon (2 ml) ground cumin
½ teaspoon (2 ml) ground ginger
⅛ teaspoon (0.5 ml) ground cloves

TOPPING:
⅓ cup (75 ml) heavy cream (36%)
⅓ cup (75 ml) ghee
½ cup (125 ml) finely shaved jaggery
½ cup (125 ml) flaked coconut
½ cup (125 ml) almonds, chopped

1 2
3 4

1	Preheat oven to 315°F (160°C). Line the bottom of a 9-inch (24 cm) springform pan. Beat the eggs and sugar until thick.	2	Fold in the ghee and yogurt and mix to combine.	
3	Sift together the flour, baking powder, baking soda, salt and spices. Fold the dry ingredients into the egg mixture.	4	Pour the mixture into the prepared pan and bake for 45 minutes.	➤

| 5 | Combine the topping ingredients and spread over the top of the cake. | **NOTES**
❋
You can substitute butter for the ghee, using exactly the same quantity. However, the cake will no longer be Ayurvedic in nature, as butter has different properties to ghee and doesn't have the same medicinal qualities. |

| 6 | Bake for a further 20 minutes. Allow to cool in the pan for 10 minutes before running a knife around the rim to release from the pan. Serve warm with yogurt. | **TIP** ❋
This cake will keep in an airtight container for up to 3 days, but the topping may soften slightly. |

MASALA CHAI

❧ MAKES 4 CUPS (1 L) • PREPARATION: 15 MINUTES • COOKING: 15 MINUTES ❧

Ayurvedic

6 green cardamom pods, lightly crushed
6 black peppercorns
2 cinnamon sticks, broken in half
4 whole cloves
1 teaspoon (5 ml) fennel seeds
1 tablespoon (15 ml) sliced fresh ginger or
   1 teaspoon (5 ml) ground ginger

2 teaspoons (10 ml) Assam tea leaves or
2 Assam tea bags
1 cup (250 ml) unhomogenized milk
2 tablespoons (30 ml) grated jaggery or soft
   brown sugar

NOTE:
This is a warming tea, great for winter. Adjust the spices in summer, or if you tend to have Pitta heat issues, by reducing the amount of cinnamon and omitting the peppercorns and ginger. Subsitute with dried rose petals.

1 2
3 4

1	Put the spices in a pot, add the water and bring to a boil. Reduce the heat and simmer for 5 minutes.	2	Add the tea leaves or tea bags and bring back to a boil.
3	As soon as the tea boils, add the milk and sugar and bring back to a boil. Reduce the heat and simmer for 5 minutes.	4	Strain, reserving the spices and tea, which can be used up to three more times. Serve hot.

BANANA LASSI + VATA TEA

❖ SERVES 4 • PREPARATION: 15 MINUTES • COOKING: 10 MINUTES ❖

BANANA LASSI
Put 1 cup (250 ml) plain yogurt, 2 cups (500 ml) water, 1 chopped banana, brown sugar (to taste) and 1 teaspoon (5 ml) rosewater in a blender or food processor and blend until smooth and creamy.

VATA TEA
Put 1 tablespoon (15 ml) finely grated ginger, 1 cinnamon stick, 4 whole cloves, 1 teaspoon (5 ml) fennel seeds and 1 tablespoon (15 ml) brown sugar in a pot. Pour boiling water on top and let brew for 5 minutes.

PITTA + KAPHA TEAS

❧ SERVES 4 • PREPARATION: 15 MINUTES • COOKING: 10 MINUTES ❧

PITTA TEA
Put 1 teaspoon (5 ml) fennel seeds, 1 teaspoon (5 ml) coriander seeds, 4 lightly crushed green cardamom pods, 1 teaspoon (5 ml) finely grated ginger, 2 tablespoons (30 ml) torn mint leaves and 1 tablespoon (15 ml) grated jaggery (optional) in a teapot. Pour boiling water on top and let brew for 5 minutes.

KAPHA TEA
Put 1 tablespoon (15 ml) finely grated ginger, 1 teaspoon (5 ml) fenugreek seeds, 4 whole cloves, ¼ teaspoon (1 ml) turmeric and ¼ teaspoon (1 ml) black peppercorns in a teapot. Pour boiling water on top and let brew for 5 minutes.

Ayurvedic

APPENDIXES

GLOSSARY

Ajowan: Also called ajwain, these are small brown seeds that have a fresh thyme-like flavor and are used to flavor vegetable dishes and savory flatbreads.

Amchoor: Dried green mango powder that adds a sour flavor to curries, fish and meat dishes.

Asafetida: Also known as hing, it is a pungent strong-smelling spice used to add a garlic-like flavor to dishes. Store in the freezer and seal well or you will learn the hard way — this stuff stinks.

Atta flour: This type of flour is the main whole wheat flour used to make naan, poori and chapati. It is made from a certain type of hard wheat that is high in gluten. The gluten gives it an elastic quality and makes it perfect for rolling into thin breads.

Besan: Also called gram flour, this is a golden-colored flour made from ground chickpeas. It is used in Indian cooking to make batters or to coat foods before deep-frying, and it has a rich nutty flavor. It thickens on standing, so if a batter looks a little thin, set it aside for about 15 minutes to thicken.

Brown cardamom pods: Also called black cardamom, these are large brown wrinkled seeds, about ¾ inch (2 cm) in length, that look like small nutmeg seeds. They are added whole to meat, chicken and vegetable dishes in northern India. They have a wonderful smoky, aromatic flavor, but use sparingly as too much can easily overpower a meal. They are not a substitute for green cardamom pods.

Black Indian salt: Also called kala namak, it is a pink mineral salt widely used in Indian and Ayurvedic cooking. It has a strong, sulfurous odor and is valued for its high mineral content. It is a major ingredient in chaat masala (see below).

Black mustard seeds: Tiny black seeds that form the base of most southern Indian dishes. Cook in a little hot oil until they pop, then continue cooking your dish. They are sometimes cooked in a tarka (a spice mix) and poured over a dal at the end of cooking.

Chaat masala: A spiced salt mix that is used on fruit, potatoes and vegetable dishes. It also sprinkled over snacks, which are known as chaat in India.

Chana dal: Split peas that are golden in color and need to be soaked in water to soften before using. They can be blended after soaking and used to thicken mixtures or bind ground meat.

Chickpeas: Also called garbanzo beans, these cream-colored legume are probably the only type of chickpea known to people who don't have a lot of experience with Indian cooking. They are used in Muslim-style Indian dishes, such as chole. Dried beans need to be soaked overnight before cooking. They are also ground to make flour.

Chili powder: It can vary in both color and spiciness. Kashmiri chili powder is often used in Indian cooking, as it is the reddest of all the chili powders but is not too spicy. Hot chili powder is usually made from small bird's eye chilies and is very potent, so be careful when using it.

Coconut milk: You can purchase canned coconut milk or cream, or you can purchase coconut milk powder and make your own. The latter will give you a product closer to the coconut milk they make in India. Follow the instructions on the package for the quantities to use, as it will vary depending on the brand.

Curry leaves: Small green aromatic leaves that add a distinctive curry flavor to southern Indian dishes. Fry in a little oil at the beginning of a dish. Fresh is best if you can find them; they will freeze quite well.

Dal: The name given to beans and pulses in India and also the name used for the cooked dish.

Dried fenugreek leaves: These leaves are also known as katsuri methi leaves and are usually added toward the end of cooking. Their slightly bitter flavor is great for cutting through rich, creamy dishes. Use in moderation as their flavor can overpower a dish.

Ghee: Clarified butter, made by heating butter to remove the milky solids. Ghee may be heated to high temperatures without burning, unlike butter. It is widely used in Indian and Ayurvedic cooking. Ayurveda regards homemade ghee to be extremely nourishing for all doshas, but Kaphas should use it in moderation.

Green cardamom: Bright-green elongated pods that are filled with small black seeds. The brighter the pod, the better the quality of the spice. Lightly crush the pod with a mortar and pestle to release the flavor. Green cardamom pods have a pungent aroma and are most often used in sweet recipes.

Green chilies: Indian green chilies are bright green and are fairly hot. If you would like to temper the spiciness of a dish, remove the chili seeds and white membrane before using it in the recipe.

Jaggery: This is an unrefined sugar usually made from sugarcane, although it can also be made from the sap of the date or coconut palm. It is most often sold in rectangular blocks and can be grated or shaved directly from the block. You can find it in Asian grocery stores and other specialty food stores.

Kala chana: Bengal gram beans, also called black chickpeas, are the most widely used chickpeas in India. They have a wonderful creamy, nutty texture and can be fried and served as a snack or added to curries or soups or made into dals. The ground beans are used to make flour, which is widely used in India to make pakoras (vegetables covered in batter and deep-fried) or batters for deep-frying.

Nigella: Also called black onion seeds or kalonji seeds, these tiny pointed black seeds are added to breads or naan to add a slight onion flavor.

Mung dal: Split mung beans are small green oval-shaped bean that sheds its skin when cooked and acquires a creamy texture. It is often used in dals and soups. It is one of the most easily digested of the dals and is suitable for Vata, Pitta and Kapha doshas. Soak dried beans before cooking.

Paneer: A fresh cheese made from cow's milk that has been curdled using lemon juice or vinegar. The whey is discarded, and the curds are drained in cheesecloth to create the cheese. It has a soft texture, but it can be weighed down and thereby becomes quite firm. Paneer has a mild, milky flavor and will keep chilled in an airtight container for 3 to 4 days.

Rajma: The name given to both the red kidney beans and the dish that is cooked with them. The dried beans need to be soaked in cold water overnight before using.

Masoor dal: Red lentils that are widely available in supermarkets and require no soaking. They are best used in combination with richer beans (such as split mung beans or black gram beans) to make dals and soups.

Sambar powder: This is a spice blend that includes besan. It is used to make a spicy lentil and vegetable broth that is ladled over rice, and it can also be added to batters or pakora mixes.

Semolina: Semolina is made from ground wheat. You can buy fine or coarse semolina; the fine will give you a thin porridge while the coarse can be used to make chow chow bhath and upma.

Split mung dal: Split mung beans with the husks removed. They are golden colored and slightly flat. Perfect for making dals, thickening soups or adding to batters and doughs. They require no soaking and cook a lot quicker than other dals. If you can't find it you could substitute split orange lentils, but you won't get the wonderful velvety smooth dal that the split mung dal will give.

Tamarind: One of the main souring agents used in Indian cooking (the other is lemon juice). Take a walnut-sized piece of tamarind pulp and place it in a jug, pour over ½ cup (125 ml) boiling water and stir to form a thick, pulpy liquid. Strain and press the pulp to remove all the liquid. Reserve the water and discard the pulp.

Toor dal: Yellow split lentils, also called split pigeon peas. They are slightly larger than chana dal but very similar in color and taste. Use in soups, sambars, dals, curries and simmered dishes. Soak the dried lentils before cooking.

MENUS

DINNER PARTY 1 — VEGETARIAN

APPETIZER
Pea & cilantro dumplings 16
MAIN
Malai kofta 30
Mung beans with coconut............................ 34

Garlic-ginger eggplant..................................... 25
Rice.. 7
DESSERT
Carrot halvah... 78

DINNER PARTY 2 — FISH & SEAFOOD

APPETIZER
Aloo tikki 15
MAIN
Goan fish 54
Shrimp curry 52

Stuffed okra.. 29
Eggplant korma 35
Rice.. 7
DESSERT
Vermicelli pudding.. 82

DINNER PARTY 3 — MEAT 1

APPETIZER
Vegetable & paneer samosas 12
MAIN
Spiced leg of lamb 38
Indian baked vegetables 31

Stuffed paratha.. 61
DESSERT
Spiced almond cookies 81
DRINKS
Masala chai.. 84

DINNER PARTY 4 — MEAT 2

APPETIZER
Vegetable & paneer kebabs.............................. 36
MAIN
Madras beef & dal curry.................................. 44
Cauliflower & spinach curry 37

Spinach dal 18
Rice.. 7
DESSERT
Mung bean pancakes 79

AYURVEDIC MENUS

All vegetarian and suitable for Vata, Pitta & Kapha

MENU 1

BREAKFAST
Chow chow bhath 11

LUNCH
Spinach dal 18
Rice 7

DINNER
Khichdi 64

DESSERT
Vermicelli pudding 82

DRINKS
Masala chai or dosha teas .... 84 & 85

MENU 2

BREAKFAST
Paneer omelet 17

LUNCH
Poha 14
Cabbage salad 76

DINNER
Rajma 21
Chapati 59

DESSERT
Carrot halvah 78

DINNER PARTY 1 — WINTER

APPETIZER
Carrot & coconut soup 10

MAIN
Stuffed paratha 61
Aloo gobi 28

Chole 19

DESSERT
Chewy spiced yogurt cake 83

DRINKS
Masala chai 84

DINNER PARTY 2 — SUMMER

APPETIZER
Butternut squash sambar 9

MAIN
Indian baked vegetables 31
Palak paneer 32

Chapati 59

DESSERT
Pistachio & mango kulfi 80

DRINKS
Dosha teas 85

AYURVEDA
HOW TO DETERMINE YOUR DOSHA

Ayurveda is an Indian traditional medicine that is over 5,000 years old. It is one of the only medical systems that treats the person rather than the disease. In Ayurveda, if you are sick it is usually because your dosha is out of balance, so to return to health you must learn how to balance your dosha.

According to Ayurveda, the universe is made up of five elements: air, space, water, earth and fire. These elements affect both our physical and mental capacities. A dosha is a mind/body type, and there are three doshas that make up our constitution: Vata, Pitta and Kapha. The doshas are made up of the elements Vata: air and space, Pitta: fire and water, and Kapha: earth and water. Very rarely is a person just one dosha; most often they are a combination of two. In a perfect world we would be a balance of all three, and that is what we should be working toward.

To determine your dosha you can go through the table opposite and tick the boxes that apply to you. It is important you do this twice. Firstly, go through and ask the question but apply it to yourself before the age of 15. This will help determine your *prakriti* — your dosha. Then go through and answer the questions — how your body is at this moment. This will determine your *vikriti* — your imbalance at this point in your life. So a person may have had a lean body frame, fiery red hair, suffered from acne and been extremely driven up to the age of 40 (Vatta Pitta prakriti). After having had children, working a sedentary and unsatisfying job, and no exercise, they have become overweight, prone to asthma and chest infections and have a high cholesterol level (Kapha, meaning vikriti is out of balance).

People are often so keen to learn their dosha — who they are — that they overlook their vikriti. Most people living in the Western world will be likely to have a Vata vikriti, as we lead fast-paced lives, consume a lot of raw or light foods, drink too much alcohol and sweet beverages and spend far too many hours in front of a computer or the TV. Those working in high-powered jobs may have a Pitta vikriti, meaning they suffer from too much heat in the body, which is a symptom of a highly driven, competitive work environment, drinking too much alcohol, an addiction to intensely flavored food, especially salty, heating Asian meals, and a desire to spend their downtime exercising in the sunshine.

Ayurveda treats the physical, mental and environmental conditions in a person's life, but, unlike other medicines, it is not up to a doctor to heal you — it is your responsibility. Only you can decide what you put in your mouth, how your spend your time and where you work and live. Ayurveda is a way of life that is based on the elements. It asks that we live in harmony with our surroundings and notice who we are and how we feel as the weather changes. It supports eating in season and encourages us to find balance in ourselves and all that we do.

I hope you will find the following information helpful. Start slowly and don't worry if you don't follow things exactly; just do your best. Photocopy the food charts and take them with you when you go shopping. Plant some of the herbs and vegetables in your garden. Follow the recipes that are marked as Ayurvedic recipes here in this book. Experiment with spices that are cherished in Ayurveda as forms of medicine. Cumin helps aid digestion, turmeric helps heal wounds, cilantro and mint will cool you down, cardamom and cinnamon will warm you up — and the list goes on and on. Ghee — oh wonderful ghee, please make it and use it — is a medicine of the gods. It might just calm your children if they are having trouble sleeping, help ease anxieties from which you may be suffering. Try it — you will only know if it works for you. It has worked for me. And milk, so many people have an aversion to this wonderful food — I did too. That was until I learned that you need to warm it and that you need to buy pasteurized, unhomogenized milk — a more digestible dairy product. Again, try it to see if it works for you.

	VATA	PITTA	KAPHA
FRAME	thin	moderate	thick
WEIGHT	low	moderate	overweight
NAILS	dry, brittle, rough, break easily	pink, soft, tender, flexible	thick, strong, oily, polished
HAIR	black, brown, knotted, thin, dry, kinky, brittle	soft, oily, yellow, blond, early gray, red, bald	thick, oily, wavy, dark or light
EYES	small, dull, dry, brown, sunken, nervous	sharp, penetrating, green, gray, yellow, sensitive to light	big, attractive, blue, calm, loving
LIPS	dry, cracked, black/brown tinge	red, inflamed, yellowish	smooth, oily, pale, whitish
TONGUE	cracked, tremors	pink, yellow	white
NOSE	slight, crooked, uneven	sharp, pointed, red tip	wide, button
TEETH	protruded, big and crooked, gums emaciated	moderate in size, yellowish, soft gums	strong, white
NECK	thin, tall	medium	big, folded
CHEST	flat, sunken	moderate	expanded, round
BELLY	flat, thin, sunken	moderate	big, potbellied
HIPS	slender, thin	moderate	heavy, big
JOINTS	cold, cracking	moderate	large, lubricated
SKIN	dry, rough, cool, brown, black	soft, oily, yellow, fair, red, yellowish, hot	thick, oily, cool, pale, white
APPETITE	variable, scant	good, excessive, angry when hungry	slow but steady
TASTE	sweet, sour, salty	sweet, bitter, astringent	pungent, bitter, astringent
THIRST	variable	excessive	scant, sparse
DIGESTION	irregular, forms gas	quick, causes burning	prolonged, forms mucus
BOWEL MOVEMENTS	dry, hard, constipated	soft, oily, loose	thick, oily, heavy, slow, sluggish
PHYSICAL ACTIVITY	very active, hyperactive	moderate	lethargic, sedentary
BODY TEMPERATURE	cool	hot	cool
PULSE	thready, feeble, moves like a snake	moderate, jumps like a frog	broad, slow, moves like a swan
TEMPERAMENT/ EMOTIONS	fearful, insecure, unpredictable, anxious, flexible, fickle	aggressive, intelligent, irritable, anger, hate, jealousy, determined	calm, slow, greedy, attached, loyal, possessive
CONTROL OF EMOTIONS	gets upset but forgets easily	gets angry, can hold emotions in	takes a lot to upset, withdraws
CONCENTRATION	difficult to concentrate	intense	methodical
MENTAL ACTIVITY	always active	moderate	dull, slow
MEMORY	quick to learn, quick to forget	learns quickly	slow to learn, never forgets
SPEECH	rapid, unclear	sharp, penetrating	slow, monotonous
SLEEP	scant, broken up, sleeplessness	little but sound	deep, prolonged
DREAMS	quick, active, many, fearful, flying, jumping, running	fiery, anger, violence, war	watery, rivers, oceans, lakes, swimming, snow, romantic
FAITH	changeable	fanatic	steady, faith based on love
SPENDING	poor, spends quickly and doesn't remember what on	moderate, spends money on luxury items	rich, money saver, spends on food

KAPHA FOODS

Kapha individuals tend to be heavyset and often experience problems with their weight when they are out of balance. They are calm, caring and compassionate and possess incredible stamina. Kaphas have a strong constitution and tend to live longer than the other doshas.

Elements that dominate this dosha: water and earth.

Elements that aggravate this dosha: water and earth.

Elements that decrease/calm: fire, air and space.

Tastes that aggravate this dosha: sweet, sour, salty.

Tastes that calm this dosha: bitter, pungent, astringent.

Signs that Kapha is out of balance in the body: lethargy, laziness, difficulty getting out of bed after a good night's sleep, unmotivated, depression, fluid retention. You have begun to isolate yourself and withdraw from friends. You become greedy and attached. Kaphas might find themselves overeating or eating for comfort, especially sweet or fatty foods. Weight gain, diabetes, oily skin and hair, heavy, congested feeling in the chest and lungs, excess mucus, asthma, excessive sweet cravings and tender breasts before menstruation are other symptoms you may experience.

Habits and lifestyle factors that imbalance this dosha: eating too many sweet foods (this includes fruit); eating cold, white, damp foods (especially ice cream, milk and yogurt); excess dairy in the diet; too much alcohol or sweet drinks; overeating (especially in the evening before bed), overexposure to cold damp environments; lack of exercise; sleeping during the day; going to bed with wet hair; drinking too much liquid, be it water or hot drinks; sitting around doing nothing for long periods at a time.

Activities that will balance Kapha: vigorous exercise, especially in the morning between 6:00 a.m. and 10:00 a.m.; running; cycling; aerobic activity; and competitive sports. Learning a new skill, stimulating the mind and changing or varying your daily routine will keep you from feeling stuck and bogged down. Travel, seek out new friendships and meet new people, which will help you get out of your comfort zone. Have your main meal at lunchtime.

Site of Kapha in the body: chest, lungs, throat, head, sinuses, nose, mouth and tongue, bones, plasma and mucus are where Kapha will present more strongly when it is out of balance.

Time of day: 6:00 a.m. to 10:00 a.m and 6:00 p.m. to 10:00 p.m are the times of day when Kapha will be more obvious in the body and mind.

Time of year: winter is the time of year when Kapha can be more aggravated in the body.

Time of life: 0 to 13 years is the time when Kapha will be more prominent in the body.

Responsible for: compassion, loyalty, patience, forgiveness, body structure (bones, muscles, tendons, ligaments) and stability. lubrication, protection, strength, firmness of the body, maintenance of bodily fluids, groundedness and long-term memory.

ATTRIBUTES OF THE KAPHA INDIVIDUAL — HOW THEY MANIFEST IN THE BODY

Heavy: Kaphas have heavy bones and solid frames, bulky muscles and can be overweight. They have calm, deep voices and are usually quite grounded in mind and body.

Slow/Dull: They can tend to be slow to react. They walk and speak slowly and only after allowing time to think about what they are going to say. Kapha have a sluggish metabolism.

Cool: They have cold, clammy skin. They often get a cold, cough or congestion. They are drawn to cooling, sweet foods.

Oily: They have soft, oily skin, hair and feces and well-lubricated joints.

Liquid: Kaphas tend to have a problem with fluid retention, congestion in their chest, nose and throats and excess mucus. This can be very obvious in young children with runny noses.

Smooth: They are blessed with soft, smooth alabaster-like skin and a smooth, calm nature.

Dense: Kaphas have thick hair, nails, skin and muscles.

Soft: They have soft, doe-like eyes and a very soft, caring nature, which makes them extremely forgiving.

Static: This, unfortunately, can make them very happy to just sit around or sleep for long periods of time.

Sticky: They can have a tendency to become quite attached to things they care about.

Cloudy: Kaphas can have a foggy mind in the morning, and they can also take a while to understand things at the best of times.

Hard: This quality gives them firm muscles and strength in both mind and body.

Gross: Kaphas can suffer from fatty tissue, blockages and obesity.

Sweet: Kaphas have a sweet nature. They are also drawn to sweet foods, which can cause them to become unbalanced.

Salty: Salty tastes will assist in digestion. However, too much salt can lead to fluid retention, and this can often be a problem for Kaphas.

White: Kaphas have a pale complexion, and they love white foods, especially dairy. They tend to have white mucus and a white coating on their tongue when they are out of balance.

KAPHA FOOD CHART

FOOD	FAVOR	AVOID
FRUITS	Apples, apricots, berries, cherries, dried fruits, grapes, kiwis, lemons,* limes,* mangoes,* oranges,* peaches, pears, persimmons, pomegranates, quinces, raisins, strawberries,* tangerines,* tamarind*	**Excessively sweet, sour or watery fruits, such as** avocados, bananas, coconut, cranberries, dates, fresh figs, grapefruit, melons, papayas, pineapple, plums, rhubarb, soursop, watermelon
VEGETABLES	**Pungent bitter vegetables, such as** asparagus, eggplant, beet and greens, broccoli, cabbage, carrots, cauliflower, celery, corn, green beans, leafy greens, mushrooms, onions, peas, peppers, white potatoes, spinach,* sprouts, winter squash, cooked tomato	**Sweet and juicy vegetables:** Cucumber, olives (black or green), parsnips,# sweet potato, pumpkin, summer squashes, raw tomatoes, zucchini
GRAINS	Amaranth,* barley, bran, buckwheat, corn, granola, millet, oats (dry), quinoa	Bread (with yeast), cooked oats, pasta,# basmati rice,* brown and white rice, rice cakes,# rye, wheat
LEGUMES	All lentils, black beans, chickpeas, mung beans,* navy beans, peas (dried), pinto beans, soy milk, tempeh, tofu (hot)	Kidney beans, miso, soybeans, soy cheese, soy sauce, tofu (cold)
DAIRY	Buttermilk,* cottage cheese,* ghee,* goat's cheese (unsalted and not aged), goat's milk (skimmed), yogurt	Butter (salted), butter (unsalted),* cheese (most), cow's milk, ice cream, sour cream, yogurt (plain, with fruit or frozen), dairy — if you do want to eat dairy opt for lower-fat dairy products.
NUTS & SEEDS	Flaxseed (linseed),* pumpkin,* sunflower*	Almonds,# all other nuts, coconut,# psyllium,# sunflower*
MEATS, FISH & SEAFOOD	Chicken (white meat), eggs (not fried), freshwater fish, shrimp, rabbit, turkey (white meat), venison	Beef, chicken (dark meat), saltwater fish, lamb, mutton, pork, turkey
SWEETENERS	Fruit juice concentrate, raw honey — 1 tablespoon (15 ml) a day helps to release Kapha, but do not heat the honey	Barley malt, maple syrup, molasses, natural sugar, white sugar
SPICES	All pungent, bitter and astringent spices are good for Kapha, especially asafetida, chili pepper/cayenne, ginger, mustard seeds (both black and yellow) and turmeric	Salt
CONDIMENTS	Black pepper, chilies, horseradish, mustard, scallions, seaweed*	Chocolate, lime, mayonnaise, pickles, salt, vinegar
OILS	**For external and internal use in small amounts:** Corn, canola, sesame, sunflower (external)	All oils that are not in the favor column; use only small amounts of extra-virgin olive oil, ghee, mustard oil and safflower oil
BEVERAGES	Dry wine,* apple juice/cider,* carob, cranberry juice, grain coffee, grape juice, pineapple juice,* pomegranate juice, prune juice, soy milk (if hot and well spiced)	Beer, hard spirits, sweet wine, almond milk, caffeinated beverages,# chocolate milk, grapefruit juice, iced tea, icy cold drinks, orange juice, rice milk, tomato juice
HERB TEAS	Herb teas (see recipe 85) throughout the day, black tea (if well spiced), chamomile, cinnamon, fennel,* peppermint, yerba maté; Kapha tea (see recipe 85) throughout the day to pacify Kapha; drink two cups of ginger tea a day to help stimulate digestion	Licorice,* marshmallow, rosehip#

Key: *moderation; #occasionally

PITTA FOODS

Pitta individuals are dominated by the element of fire, which creates heat in the body and is responsible for metabolizing, transforming and processing all of our thoughts, emotions, sensory perceptions and the food we eat. Pitta is also in charge of maintaining our digestive fire ("agni"). If our digestive fire is low we will have problems with digestion and suffer from heartburn, reflux and indigestion. Pittas have quick, sharp minds and tongues, a moderate body frame and tend to be able to maintain their weight better than the other two doshas.

Elements that dominate this dosha: fire and water.

Elements that aggravate this dosha: fire.

Elements that decrease/calm this dosha: air, water, earth.

Tastes that aggravate this dosha: salty, sour, pungent.

Tastes that calm this dosha: sweet, bitter, astringent.

Signs that Pitta is out of balance in the body: irritability, impatience, anger, pushiness, aggressiveness, skin irritations, rashes, heartburn, reflux, peptic ulcers, headaches, eye problems, hair falling out, early graying, hot flashes, loose and oily bowel movements, waking up in the middle of the night and unable to get back to sleep, excess sweating, acne, bloodshot eyes, heavy periods, large clots and extreme hunger before menstruation.

Habits and lifestyle factors that imbalance this dosha: eating too much hot, spicy, pungent, salty or sour food; excess meat in the diet; too much alcohol; overanalyzing; overworking; overexposure to heat and sun; time pressure; deadlines; intense conversations; pushing oneself too hard; emotional trauma; holding emotions in; skipping meals or fasting; exercising outside in the sun in the middle of the day in the summer; not rinsing off salt water after swimming.

Activities that will balance Pitta: eating when hungry rather than when you are starving, gentle and calming exercise, spending time in nature, being by the water, moonlight walks, yoga, dance, noncompetitive sports, swimming, gardening, writing, massage with coconut oil (as it is cooling), meditation, expressing emotions, getting to bed before 10 p.m., staying cool, cooling herbal teas.

Site of Pitta in the body: eyes, skin, stomach, small intestine, sweat glands, blood and fat are where pitta will present more strongly when it is out of balance.

Time of day: 10:00 a.m. to 2:00 p.m. and 10:00 p.m. to 2:00 a.m. are the times of day when Pitta will be more obvious in the body and mind.

Time of year: summer is the time of year when Pitta can be more aggravated in the body.

Time of life: 13 to 50 years is the time when Pitta will be more prominent in the body.

Responsible for: regulating body heat through the metabolism of food, appetite, energy production, vitality, ambition, confidence, courage, learning, understanding, creation of hunger and thirst, luster of eyes and skin, recognition, discrimination and reasoning.

ATTRIBUTES OF THE PITTA INDIVIDUAL — HOW THEY MANIFEST IN THE BODY

Hot: Pittas have strong digestive fire, which means they can usually eat a lot, and, often, they tend to get irate if they try to go without food when hungry. They tend to have a higher body temperature than other doshas and can become quite agitated in the heat.

Sharp: They can have pointed, sharp teeth, either side of their front teeth and sharp, piercing eyes. Their features are strong and distinct and quite angular. Pitta's minds are quick and extremely sharp. They are blessed with a strong memory, but their speech can be cutting. They tend to work in short, sharp bursts and can become irritable if overworked. When they suffer from pain it is usually hot and piercing.

Light: Their frame is usually light to medium. Because Pitta rules the eyes, they can also suffer from an intolerance to bright lights. Their skin is light and lustrous.

Liquid: The liquid attribute is demonstrated in Pitta's waste products: loose and light oily stools and excess sweat and urine. They usually have a greater thirst than other doshas.

Spreading: This can be seen in the form of skin rashes, acne, inflammation and heat that moves in the body. Pittas like to be well known and want their name to be spread all over the world.

Oily: They have soft, oily skin and hair. They may find it difficult to digest deep-fried foods.

Sour: Pittas can often experience stomach acid, increased reflux and excess salivation.

Pungent: Pittas will experience heartburn or other strong, burning feelings both physically and mentally. Their bodies may emit a pungent smell either from the mouth, armpits, feet or feces.

Bitter: They will often be left with a bitter taste in their mouths following heated exchanges. They tend to have an aversion to bitter flavors. They can become bitter and twisted if they don't get their own way.

Red: They can have fiery red hair, flushed red skin, nose and cheeks, red rashes and red skin from sunburn. Red will aggravate Pittas.

FOOD	FAVOR	AVOID
FRUITS	Sweet fruits, apples, avocado, sweet berries, coconut, fresh figs, goji berries, dark grapes, kiwi,* lemons,* limes,* mangoes, melons, oranges, pears, pineapple (sweet), plums, pomegranate, prunes, quince,* raisins, strawberries,* tamarind,* watermelon	Bananas, berries (sour), cherries (sour), cranberries, grapes (green), grapefruit, papayas, peaches, persimmons, rhubarb, soursop
VEGETABLES	**Sweet and bitter vegetables, such as** artichoke, asparagus, cooked beets,* broccoli, Brussels sprouts, cabbage, cauliflower, cooked carrots,* celery,* collard greens, corn,# cucumber, daikon,* dandelion greens, endive, green beans, Jerusalem artichokes, kale, kohlrabi,* leafy greens, leeks,* lettuce, mushrooms, okra, parsnips, peas, peppers, white potatoes, radicchio, arugula, sprouts, cooked spinach,* raw spinach,* spirulina, sweet potatoes, winter squash (acorn, butternut, spaghetti), watercress, zucchini	Eggplant,# beet (raw), horseradish, chilies, garlic, onion (raw), radish, Swiss chard, taro root, tomatoes, turnip
GRAINS	Amaranth, barley, barley flour,* bran, bulgur,* couscous,* granola, cooked oats, whole wheat pasta,* rice (basmati, brown or white), rice (medium grain or sushi),* rice cakes, udon noodles,* unbleached white flour,* wheat, whole wheat flour*	Bread (with yeast), buckwheat, corn, millet, dry oats, quinoa, rice,* rye
LEGUMES	Aduki, black beans, black-eyed peas, chickpeas, kidney beans, lentils (all but red), lima beans, mung beans (whole or split), navy beans, pinto beans, soybeans, soy cheese, soy milk, split peas (green and yellow), tempeh,* tofu, black gram beans*	Red lentils, yellow split peas
DAIRY	Butter (unsalted), cheese (fresh, soft but not aged, unsalted), cottage cheese, cow's milk (unhomogenized), ghee, goat's milk, ice cream,* yogurt (fresh and diluted with a little water),* yogurt (sweetened)	Butter (salted), buttermilk, cheese (hard), feta cheese, goat's cheese, labneh, Parmesan cheese, sour cream, yogurt (plain, with fruit or frozen)
NUTS & SEEDS	Almonds (soaked overnight and peeled), coconut, flaxseed (linseed), pumpkin seeds,* pysllium, sunflower	All nuts, sesame seeds (black and white), tahini
MEAT, FISH & SEAFOOD	Chicken (white meat), egg whites, freshwater fish, shrimp,* rabbit, turkey (white meat), venison	Beef, chicken (dark meat), egg yolks, saltwater fish, lamb, mutton, pork, turkey (dark meat)
SWEETENERS	Amasake (rice milk),* barley malt, brown sugar, fructose, fruit juice concentrates, dates, honey,* jaggery, maple syrup, rice syrup, unrefined brown rice syrup,* whole can sugar (Sucanat)	Molasses, sugar substitutes, white sugar
HERBS, SPICES & FLAVORINGS	Fresh basil,* caraway,* cardamom,* cinnamon,* cilantro, cumin, curry leaves, fresh dill, dill seed,* fennel, fresh ginger,* garam masala,* nutmeg,* kudzu, mint, peppermint, parsley,* saffron, tamarind,* turmeric, vanilla*	Ajowan, allspice, amchoor (mango powder), anise, asafetida (hing), bay leaf, black pepper,* cayenne, chili powder, cloves, fenugreek, garlic, ginger (dry), marjoram, miso, mustard seeds, nutmeg, oregano, paprika, pippali (long pepper), rosemary, thyme, sage
CONDIMENTS	Coconut (grated or milk), ginger (sweet pickled),* gomashio (mild), herb,* mint (chopped), mirin,* olives,* lime,* rock salt,* rosewater, seaweed* (soak and rinse before using), sea salt,* tamari,* vinegar	Chili peppers, chocolate, gomasio, ketchup, miso, mustard, mayonnaise (commercial), pickles (sour), salt (iodized), sauerkraut, soy sauce, vinegar
OILS	**For internal and external use:** Ghee, canola, coconut, olive (external), soybean, sunflower	Almond, animal fats or lard, apricot, avocado,# blended vegetable oils, corn, mustard, nut oils, safflower, sesame
BEVERAGES	Beer,# dry white wine,# almond milk,* aloe vera juice, apple juice, apricot juice, berry juice (sweet), carob, carrot juice,* coconut milk, coconut water, cow's milk,* dandelion, grape juice, lassi,* mango juice, orange juice,* peach juice, pear juice, pomegranate juice, prune juice, rice milk, soy milk*	Spirits, red wine, caffeinated beverages, chocolate milk, cranberry juice, grapefruit juice, ice tea, icy cold drinks, lemonade, pineapple juice, tomato juice
HERB TEAS	Drink herb teas (see recipe 85) throughout day, alfalfa,* bancha, barley, blackberry, cardamom,* chamomile, cinnamon,* fennel, ginger (fresh),* hibiscus,* jasmine, lavender, lemon balm, licorice, marshmallow, mint, raspberry leaf, rosehip, saffron	Ajowan, cloves, corn silk, eucalyptus, ginger (dried), ginseng, pennyroyal, sage, sassafras

Key: *moderation; #occasionally

VATA FOODS

Vata individuals tend to have thin, light frames. They are quick thinkers and can be quite nervous and excitable. The vata dosha is responsible for movement and elimination of all wastes from the body. Vatas are susceptible to the cold and wind, so it is essential that they keep warm, maintain a routine and nourish themselves with warm cooked foods. Vata influences all other doshas, as it is responsible for movement, and all bodily functions that require movement to function.

Elements that dominate this dosha: air and space.

Elements that aggravate this dosha: air and space.

Elements that decrease/calm this dosha: earth, fire and water.

Tastes that aggravate this dosha: bitter, pungent, astringent.

Tastes that calm this dosha: sweet, sour, salty.

Signs that Vata is out of balance in the body: gas, constipation, anxiety, weight loss, restlessness, hypertension, arthritis, dry or cracked skin and lips, insomnia, worry, anxiety, unable to concentrate and sit still, dry or flaky scalp, problems with short-term memory.

Habits and lifestyle factors that imbalance this dosha: eating too many cold foods and icy drinks, excess raw foods (such as salads, especially in the colder months), irregular meals or skipping meals, too much travel, being outside in the cold and wind, lack of sleep and routine, spending too much time in front of the computer or TV, stress, overthinking, talking too much.

Activities that will balance Vata: gentle, calming exercise such as yoga; qigong; dance; golf; walking; swimming; listening to calming music; gardening; pottery; cooking; massage; meditation; routine.

Site of Vata in the body: nervous system, mind, bladder, waist, feet, bones and colon are where Vata will present more strongly when it is out of balance.

Time of day: 2:00 a.m. to 6:00 a.m. and 2:00 p.m. to 6:00 p.m. are the times of day when Vata will be more obvious in the body and mind.

Time of year: fall, late winter and spring are the times of year when Vata can be more aggravated in the body.

Time of life: 50 years and older is the time when Vata will be more prominent in the body.

Responsible for: joy, happiness, creativity, speech, sneezing, inhalation and exhalation, enthusiasm, circulation, digestion/peristalsis, delivery of baby, heartbeat, reflexes, tears, expression of emotions, movement and elimination.

ATTRIBUTES OF THE VATA INDIVIDUAL — HOW THEY MANIFEST IN THE BODY

Cold: Coldness appears in the hands and feet. Vatas will have a tendency to avoid cold temperatures and love warmer climates. They have poor circulation and can suffer from cold bones and stiffness.

Dry: Dryness is a major issue for Vatas. They often have dry skin, hair, lips or tongue and a husky voice. Dryness in their colon usually leads to them suffering from constipaton.

Light: Vata individuals are generally light in body weight with fine muscles and bones. They sleep lightly and wake easily, with little noise needed to disturb them.

Rough: Roughness appears in the body as cracked skin, nails, split ends on hair, cracked teeth and joints that creak and crack when moving.

Subtle: They will suffer from an underlying subtle anxiety, fear and insecurity. Vatas will also have goose bumps, muscle twitches and tremors.

Mobile: Vatas can't sit still. They walk fast, talk fast and tend to be incredible multitaskers. They are good at making money and great at spending it. Their eyes will dart around the room as they talk to you with their hands or shake their leg. They love to travel and find it difficult to stay in one place for too long. Their moods are ever-changing, as is their faith and their thoughts. Vatas love change and do what they can to make it happen often.

Clear: This quality gives Vata their clairvoyant ability; it is related to the element of space. Vatas can understand easily but forget abruptly, and they often experience a deep sense of loneliness.

Astringent: They can suffer from a dry, choking feeling in their throats, and they will often find themselves with hiccups or burping. They enjoy oily, sweet, sour and salty foods.

Brownish black: Vatas usually have a dark complexion, dark hair and small dark eyes.

VATA FOOD CHART

FOOD	FAVOR	AVOID
FRUITS	Sweet fruits, apricots, avocados, bananas, berries, cherries, coconut, dates, fresh figs, grapefruits, grapes, kiwi, lemons, limes, mango, sweet melons, oranges, papaya, peaches, pineapple, plums, raisins (soaked), rhubarb, soursop, strawberries, tamarind, tangerines	Dried fruits, apples, cranberries, pears, persimmons, pomegranates, prunes, quinces, watermelon
VEGETABLES	Cooked artichokes, asparagus, bok choy, beets, butternut squash, carrots, cucumber, daikon (mooli), fenugreek greens, green beans, horseradish, leeks, mustard greens, okra, olives, onions, parsnips, pumpkin, radish, rutabaga, squash, sweet potato, watercress, zucchini	Most frozen, dried or raw vegetables, eggplant, beet greens, broccoli, Brussels sprouts, burdock root, cabbage, cauliflower, celery, corn, Jerusalem artichokes, kohlrabi, leafy greens, lettuce, mushrooms, raw onions, parsley, peas, peppers, potatoes, spinach, sprouts, tomatoes, turnips
GRAINS	Amaranth, all rices, bulgur, cooked oats, rice flour, unbleached white flour, wheat, whole wheat flour, wild rice	Cold and dry puffed cereals, barley, buckwheat, corn, millet, dry oats, granola, oat bran, quinoa, rice cakes
LEGUMES	Azuki beans, black lentils, mung beans, red lentils, soy cheese, soy milk, tofu, toor dal	Black beans, black-eyed peas, yellow split peas, chickpeas, kidney beans, lentils, lima beans, navy beans, pinto beans, soybeans, soy flour, split peas, tempeh, white beans
DAIRY	Buttermilk, butter, cheese (fresh), cheese (hard), cow's milk (organic, unhomogenzied and raw), ghee, goat's milk, sour cream, yogurt (spiced)*	Cow's milk (powdered), goat's milk (powdered), ice cream,# yogurt (plain fruit or frozen)
NUTS & SEEDS	Almonds, Brazil nuts, cashews, chestnuts, coconut, flaxseed (linseed), hazelnuts, macadamias, peanuts,# pecans, pine nuts, pistachios, pumpkin seeds, sesame seeds, sunflower seeds, walnuts	Psyllium#
MEATS, FISH & SEAFOOD	Beef,# chicken (dark meat), turkey (dark meat), duck meat and duck eggs, eggs, fish (all), shrimp	Lamb, pork, rabbit, venison
SWEETENERS	Barley malt syrup, brown rice syrup, brown sugar (unrefined), dates, fructose, honey, jaggery, juice concentrates, maple syrup, palm sugar, raw sugar, sugar cane juice, whole can sugar (Sucanat)	White sugar, sugar substitutes, honey (cooked)
HERBS, SPICES & FLAVORINGS	Almond extract, amchoor powder (mango powder), anise, asafetida, basil, bay leaf, black pepper, caraway, cardamom, chili pepper, cilantro, cinnamon, cloves, cumin, curry powder, dill, fennel, fenugreek,* garam masala, garlic, ginger (fresh and dried), mace, mustard seeds, nutmeg, oregano, paprika, peppermint, pippali, rosemary, rosewater, saffron, sage, savory, star anise, tamarind, tarragon, thyme, turmeric, vanilla	Curry leaves (neem), garlic (raw)
CONDIMENTS	Chili peppers,* lemon, lime, mayonnaise, mustard, pickles, salt, seaweed, vinegar	Chocolate, horseradish
OILS	**For internal and external use:** Ghee, olive, sesame	Flaxseed (linseed)
BEVERAGES	Beer, white wine,* carob,* grain coffee, grape juice, lemonade, orange juice, pineapple juice, soy milk (if spiced and hot)	Spirits, red wine, apple juice, caffeinated beverages, chocolate milk, cranberry juice, ice tea, icy cold drinks, prune juice,* soy milk (cold), tomato juice*
HERB TEAS	Drink herb teas (see recipe 85) throughout the day, bancha, basil, cinnamon,* fennel, ginger, licorice, peppermint, rosehip	Dandelion, ginseng, nettle,* red clover, yerba maté

Key: *moderation; #occasionally

INDEX

ACKNOWLEDGMENTS

This is a very special book for me because it allowed me to combine my passions and put them on paper. I have been studying Ayurveda for many years, and it forms the foundation of my life, along with yoga. Ayurveda provides me with guidelines for how to keep my mind, body and spirit in balance. I don't always succeed, but I do my best.

As part of my research for this book I traveled to India and spent time with two very special women without whom this book would not have been possible. Tina Sassoon, my dear, generous, kind, creative, earth mother friend who brings joy to the tummies of thousands of yogis at her home in Gokalum near Mysore in India. Tina, thanks so much for making all you know available to me. Mani Uma, the soft, kind, compassionate, knowledgeable and truly Kapha Ayurvedic chef at Satsanga retreat in Goa. Mani's knowledge of Ayurveda was passed down from her father, and it was a joy for me to spend days in the kitchen with her, building on my knowledge and compiling a wonderful selection of delicious recipes. Thanks to Miffy for introducing me to Mani, and to Jodie and Olaf for making my stay so comfortable. Thanks to Mish Lucia for sharing a part of the epic journey with me, memorable as it was.

While I am thanking my teachers, I must not forget my rock, my inspiration, my guide and my friend Dr. Ajit, head teacher at the Australasian Institute of Ayurvedic Studies, who teaches his science with such passion, discipline, preciseness and kindness. And again none of this happens without the support of an amazing group of people in Australia. I can't just fly around the world, eating, researching, shopping and styling without those at home who mind the fort for me. Kawika Boyce, you are gold and I can never repay you for taking care of my Pridey girl as you do. Annie Mac, my gorgeous sis, for sorting out my mail and all the stuff that doesn't go away when I leave the country — wish as I might.

To those who work in the engine room with me, I am eternally grateful. Catie Ziller, my savvy publisher; Kathy Steer, my catch-me-when-I-fall-editor; and Alice Chadwick, quiet-as-a-mouse designer. And to those who sweat it out in the kitchen with me. Penellie Grieve, what a lucky one I was to have one of my dearest as my copilot testing this book, what a joy. Kirsten Jenkins, my super talented, efficient, funny, loyal, home ec for loving the food she cooked for the shoot. My über cool photographer, James Lyndsay, what a pleasure it was working with you and getting to know you. Finally to Sarah Tildesley, my beautiful friend who allows me to live, eat, work and sleep in her sunny sweet home, grateful is not enough.